A CONCISE & ILLUSTRATED
MILITARY HISTORY
OF BARBADOS
1627-2007

BY
MAJOR MICHAEL HARTLAND

The photograph on the cover is of the Main Guard on the Savannah of the Garrison Historic Area. The building, completed in 1804, is unique and is a magnificent example of British Military Architecture of the late 18th and early 19th centuries.

Note from the Publisher
Many of the photographs reproduced in this book are very old and in poor condition. As such they have not printed clearly. The author has included them because of their importance and relevance to the publication.

Published by Miller Publishing Company

Miller Publishing

Edgehill, St. Thomas, Barbados, West Indies
Tel: (246) 421-6700 or Fax: (246) 421-6701
keith@millerpublishing.net
www.BarbadosBooks.com

Graphic Design and Layout by Kristine Dear

Production coordinated by Keith Miller

Copyright © 2007 Major Michael Hartland and Miller Publishing Company

Printed in Singapore
ISBN 978 976 8215 20 8

A CONCISE & ILLUSTRATED
MILITARY HISTORY
OF BARBADOS
1627-2007

BY

MAJOR MICHAEL HARTLAND

CONTENTS

ACKNOWLEDGEMENTS

I wish to express my sincere gratitude to the following, who in various ways advised, assisted, encouraged or supported me in the completion of this book. In particular I would like to thank Mary Gleadall without whom nothing would have been achieved.

The Advocate Publishers

The Barbados Defence Force

Barbados Museum & Historical Society

The Barbados National Archives

Warren Alleyne

Cadet HQ

Don Cribbs

Paul Foster, Barbados National Trust

Florence Gittens

Penny Hynam

Felix Kerr

The Nation Publishers

Peter Tomlin

Margaret Walcott

INTRODUCTION

In September 1989, whilst serving with the Headquarters of the Barbados Defence Force, I was transferred to the newly created appointment of Garrison Secretary. I was directed to move my office into The Main Guard (the Old Savannah Club). This I did fully realizing that I was the first military person to take up residence there since the British Garrison withdrew in 1905. I not only had to co-ordinate the activities of those civilian semi-military organizations such as the Barbados Legion, The Barbados Poppy League, etc., but also to protect and promote the Garrison Historic Area. This appointment was certainly a challenge and one which I was only too happy to accept.

It soon became apparent to me that Barbados had an unparalleled military history for such a small island. Stuck in the Atlantic, a hundred miles to the East of the main stream of the Caribbean Islands, it measures only 21 miles in length and 14 miles in width at the widest point, about 166 square miles. So what was its military secret? The English soon realized that if you held Barbados you strategically held the key to the rest of the Caribbean. In a heavily laden sailing ship with the prevailing easterly winds and the strong currents and seas, you could reach the islands in a few days. To do it the other way round was virtually impossible, as the French found out to their regret.

Besides this, Barbados was becoming a very wealthy island with the advent of sugar and much of this wealth filtered down to the exchequer in England. Barbados was not to be overrun by any enemy at any cost. In 1657 Ligon, the historian described the island as a potent colony "able to muster 10,000 Foot ... and a 1,000 good horse". And later George Washington referred to it as one entire fortress. From 1627 until the present day no enemy has put foot on Barbadian soil. It was important to me to find out why. In the following pages I have listed the important dates in chronological order and then enlarged on them by the use of available prints, photographs, maps and interesting contemporary comments.

Major Michael Hartland

MAP OF THE CARIBBEAN

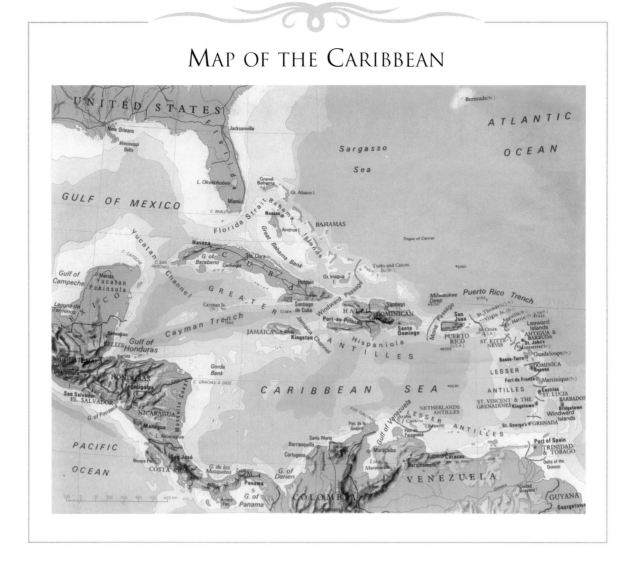

Distance in miles from Barbados

Antigua	310 miles
Belize	1,900 miles
Cayman Islands	1,500 miles
Dominica	190 miles
Grenada	150 miles
Guyana	470 miles
Hispaniola	900 miles
Jamaica	1,200 miles
Martinique	150 miles
Puerto Rico	570 miles
St. Kitts	350 miles
St. Lucia	110 miles
St. Vincent	110 miles
Tobago	150 miles
Trinidad	200 miles

MAP OF BARBADOS

CHAPTER ONE

FIRST SETTLERS ARRIVE
MILITIA FORMED
1627 - 1651

In January 1627 a vessel called the *William and John* of 100 tons commanded by Captain Powell left London with some forty emigrants, all men, who were going to plant in Barbados. She arrived off Barbados at the end of February 1627. Most of these men would have been armed with swords, muskets and small round shot with powder. They established themselves at what was known as "The Hole" and eventually "Holetown". They were soon followed by other armed settlers and the first fort was built and named Plantation Fort. The King's Colour was raised and two guns off the ships mounted there. However, although settlers were arriving in great numbers, it was not until 1646 that the Governor gave his consent to the raising of a Militia Regiment by the Royalists (Cavaliers). In 1642 the Civil War in England had started. This war was fought between those that supported the King (Cavaliers) and those that supported Parliament (Roundheads). In 1649 the King's Army was defeated and Oliver Cromwell installed himself as head of state. The majority of colonists were Cavaliers fleeing from the retribution being inflicted on them by the Roundheads. At the same time many of them were hardened soldiers and added to the strength of the Militia. Charles Fort was erected in 1650 at the entrance to Carlisle Bay. In the month of February 1651, news came to Barbados that a fleet was to be sent out from England to reduce the Cavaliers to allegiance to Parliament. Straight away the Governor placed the island on a war footing. Forces of both Horse and Foot were quickly raised which were to be paid for by the colonists and kept as a standing army. The scene was set for an invasion of Barbados.

The monolith at Holetown marks the landing of first settlers at Barbados in the reign of James I
Postcard Knight & Co.

The Island of Barbados by Isaac Sailmaker, 1694.
This painting depicts what Barbados would have looked like to the early settlers.
In 1627 there would have been no buildings, no ships, no people, just trees
© *Yale Center for British Art, The Paul Mellon Collection*

17th Century Sailing Ship, The William & John
The Barbados Philatelic Bureau, 1994
Designer A. Theobald

CHAPTER TWO

BARBADOS ATTACKED
SURRENDER OF THE ISLAND
CHARTER OF BARBADOS
1651 - 1652

On 5th August 1651 Cromwell's fleet, under the command of Sir George Ayscue, left Plymouth in England, their destination Barbados. The fleet consisted of seven Men-of-War mounting 238 guns with a force of 860 soldiers and some transport ships. They arrived off Barbados on the night of 15th October 1651 and seized some twenty ships lying in Carlisle Bay. However, in the weeks that followed, the Roundheads were unable to make an effective landing owing to the strength of the local Militia. They were, however, able to enforce a strict embargo on ships entering and leaving Barbados and were dealing a severe blow to the economy of the island. On the other hand, the Cavaliers realized the effects the embargo was having on trade and the economy in general and were looking for a way out. To add to the Governor's problems, one of his most senior commanders, Colonel Modiford, made it clear that unless an agreement was reached he would turn his regiment over to the Roundheads. Faced with these problems Governor Willoughby sought a meeting with Sir George Ayscue. Sir George was also having his problems as many of the men on the ships had gone down with scurvy, a disease associated with lack of fresh fruits and vegetables. A meeting was arranged between the Cavaliers and Roundheads in the Mermaid Tavern in Oistins on 10th January 1652 and the *Charter of Barbados* (Appendix 1) was signed on the 11th of January. The Cavaliers surrendered to the Roundheads but were given very favourable terms.

Replica of the Mermaid Tavern in the National Armoury in St. Ann's Fort.
The Commonwealth Cannon of 1652 with Cromwell's Republican Arms on
it can be seen in the foreground. This gun is one of only two known to exist.

Charles 1
Stained glass windows in Parliament Buildings,
Bridgetown

Oliver Cromwell

CHAPTER THREE

BARBADOS ATTACKED
BY
DUTCH FLEET
UNDER ADMIRAL MICHIEL de RUYTER
1665

Portrait of
Admiral Michiel de Ruyter (1673)
by Hendrik Bary
The Paul Leroy Grigaut
Memorial Collection 1969.2.120 © -
The University of Michigan Museum of Art

In 1665 the English and Dutch were at war. The Dutch Admiral Michiel de Ruyter was with his fleet in the Mediterranean but was ordered back to Holland via the Caribbean to destroy as much English shipping as he could. This he did and arrived in Barbados in the early hours of the morning of 29th April 1665. His fleet consisted of twelve line of battle ships, a formidable force. By attacking Barbados from across the Atlantic he hoped to achieve complete surprise. He would have done so if only his plans had not been leaked to the British. As de Ruyter rounded the point into Carlisle Bay he would have seen at least twenty merchant vessels at anchor. His luck, he must have thought, was in! Instead the forts and guns around the Bay opened fire together with the guns from a Man-of-War and the armed merchant vessels. At the end of the engagement his fleet had been so badly mauled that he had to withdraw out of range of the guns to repair his ships. The following morning his fleet had gone and as Barbadians would say 'not to come back'! See Appendix 2 - Eyewitness report of Admiral de Ruyter's attack.

"The Battle of the Texel, 11- 21 Aug 1673"
Painting by W. van de Velde, Jnr., 1687 - © National Maritime Museum, London

Charles Fort (aerial view)

Charles Fort was built in 1650 and was the first in a series of forts built around Carlisle Bay
to deter attempted enemy landings and to protect the shipping there. Its big guns would have
certainly contributed to the damage inflicted on de Ruyter's fleet.
Sketch artist David Jones - Warren Alleyne Collection

15

CHAPTER FOUR

EVENTS OF MILITARY IMPORTANCE
EFFECTING BARBADOS
1665 - 1789

The magazine with its massive walls contiguous to St. Ann's Fort. The fort itself was completed in 1710.

The defence of Barbados was in the hands of the Militia from 1670 to 1780. From 1670 onwards the British, French, Dutch and Spanish were constantly at war over the possession of the Caribbean Islands and many changed hands. Barbados was very much involved, because of its strategic position, and the British not only used it for their military purposes, but also called on it if they required trained troops. In 1705 work started on St. Ann's Castle or Fort as it was later known, but owing to financial restrictions was not completed until 1716. It consisted of a hexagon of massive walls and was built as a back up to Charles Fort. It could also engage ships in the Bay or defend attempted landings there. Today it is the only remaining fort in Barbados with its observation tower intact. See Appendix 3 for 1780 List of Forts & Guns (Cannon) in Barbados.

In 1751 George Washington, aged 19, who later was to become the first President of the United States, arrived in Barbados. He was accompanying his ailing elder brother whom it was thought would benefit from the climate. This was the first and only time that George Washington left North America. He stayed in a house at the top of Bush Hill within what was to become a few years later, the

The observation tower in St. Ann's Fort. There was no inside staircase so the only way to reach the top was by the precarious steps on the outside.

The walls of St. Ann's Fort with some 17th century English iron cannon in the embrasures. The observation tower is in the background

George Washington at the Battle of Princetown
(portrait by Charles Willson Peale)
The Metropolitan Museum of Art -
Gift of Collis P. Huntington, 1897 (97.33)
Photograph © 2001 The Metropolitan Museum of Art

site of the British Garrison. He was a guest on many occasions of the Commanding Officer of Charles Fort and was impressed with the fortifications there. He also journeyed along the South and West Coast noting that Barbados actually was "one entire fortress". After returning to Virginia he apparently dedicated himself to the study of warfare and soldiering in general, having had no interest in the subjects prior to arriving in Barbados, and it could well be assumed that his interest was influenced by his stay in the island. It is also said that he would have had the chance to read "The Charter of Barbados" (Appendix 1) signed between the Cavaliers and Roundheads in 1652 and that he might have been influenced by the Charter when he came to write the Constitution of the United States.

In 1778 the French informed the British that they had acknowledged the independence of the thirteen British colonies in North America and therefore they were at war with Britain. Dominica, St. Vincent, St. Lucia and Grenada fell in quick succession and Tobago was already under French control. The capture of Barbados was prominent in French planning and a strong force actually set out for the island, but owing to adverse winds they were blown so far north that they seized St. Kitts instead. At this time only Jamaica, Antigua and Barbados were in British hands and it was suddenly realized that Barbados, with its strategic importance, was vulnerable. A regiment was sent out from Britain and as there was no accommodation for it, the buildings

of the Garrison, as we know them today, were started. On 19th February 1782, Admirals Rodney and Hood defeated the French fleet at the 'Battle of the Saints' and prevented any further expansion on their part. Articles of peace were signed in 28 January 1783. The British, however, did not trust French intentions and continued to send troops to Barbados and enlarge the Garrison. In 1789 the French revolution took place and relations between France and Britain once again deteriorated.

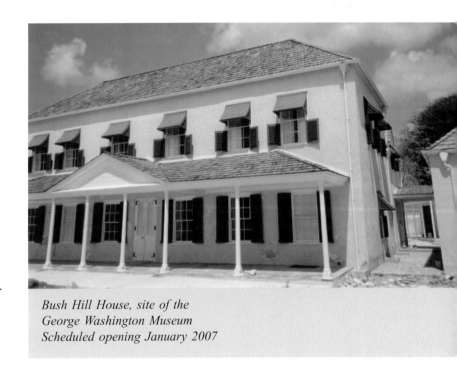

Bush Hill House, site of the George Washington Museum Scheduled opening January 2007

The Battle of the Saints - 12th April 1782
Painting by Thomas Luny © -
National Maritime Museum, London

"Admiral Sir George Brydges Rodney
1st Baron Rodney, (1719-1792)"
by Jean-Laurent Mosnier © -
National Maritime Museum, London

Admiral Samuel Hood
(1724-1816),
1st Viscount Hood
by James Northcote © -
National Maritime Museum, London

CHAPTER FIVE

THE NAPOLEONIC WARS
1793 - 1815

In 1793 Britain declared war on Revolutionary France and so began the Napoleonic Wars. Britain had been strengthening its Garrison in Barbados since 1780 and building accommodation for it. However, because of their commitments in other parts of the world, they were short of troops on the ground to recapture the French islands. In the event the British Government called for the recruitment of slaves and this was begun with the formation of two regiments, 1000 men strong, known as the West India Regiments.

Battle of Trafalgar, 21st October 1805
Nelson and HMS Victory
Joseph Mallord William Turner © -
National Maritime Museum, London,
Greenwich Hospital Collection

The officers and senior warrant officers were supplied by the British Army. By 1800 twelve regiments had been raised. The 2nd West India Regiment, recruited mainly from Barbados, played an invaluable part in the recovery of the islands and earned itself the reputation of a formidable fighting force. They were eventually to serve as part of the British Army for 120 years.

In 1802 the Treaty of Amiens brought a lull to the fighting but in 1803 all out war broke out again with the Spanish siding with the French. Between 1804 and 1810 the British, using the strategically placed island of Barbados went on the offensive retaking all the islands held by the French. Admiral Nelson's victory over the combined French and Spanish fleets in 1805 at the Battle of Trafalgar saw the end of those nations' colonial aspirations in the Caribbean.

In gratitude to Lord Nelson for removing the threat of invasion to themselves and the other Caribbean islands, the people of Barbados erected a statue in his honour in Bridgetown in 1813. The statue preceeded the one erected in Trafalgar Square in London. It is also interesting to note that the victory removed any outside threat to Barbados and the islands for the next 175 years.

Nelson's Monument,
Bridgetown, Barbados
Photo Felix Kerr

23

CHAPTER SIX
THE BUILDINGS OF THE BRITISH GARRISON

In 1780 the first British troops arrived in Barbados as a result of French aggression in the islands. There was no accommodation for them. In 1783 there was a period of peace and in 1785 the British Government decided to establish Land Forces in the Windward and Leeward Islands with Barbados as their headquarters. Construction of the buildings started in 1789 and by the early 19th century most had been completed. It was in fact the largest garrison in the Caribbean. Many of the buildings were constructed of London brick brought out as ballast in ships which returned with sugar. Some sixty of the original buildings are still in existence today as can be seen from the annotated map. (See Appendix 4 - Annotated Map of Garrison Historic Area.) There are some striking examples of British Military architecture of the time with wide verandahs and arches to keep the buildings cool.

The Military Hospital, Pavilion Court, contiguous to the Medical Pavilion, was built in 1806. It was converted into apartments in 1928.

The Medical Pavilion built in 1806 was the private residence of Senior Surgeon in charge of the Military Hospital. Reduced to a shell of a building over the years it has recently been beautifully restored.

St. Matthias Church. The foundation stone was laid in 1837 and became the Garrison Church to the British Forces and later to other local military units including the Defence Force today

*The Barbados Light & Power Building was the Commissariat Provision Store built between 1793 -1800.
Later it became the Garrison Theatre*

*This building at the top of Bush Hill was the Military Engineers Officers' Quarters.
It has been restored recently by the Barbados Turf Club*

This magnificent building, known locally as the Drill Hall, was built in 1790 onto the walls of St. Ann's Fort. Initially it was used as a barracks for soldiers and later as a commissariat.

The West India Barracks, completed in 1791, was accommodation for soldiers. It housed the West India Regiments on many occasions, hence its name.

The Stone Barracks completed by 1791 was initially accommodation for officers. It was badly damaged in the 1831 hurricane and was rebuilt as a barracks for soldiers.

The Barbados Museum was the old Military Prison and was built in 1817. It was extended in 1853 probably due to the increase in "conduct unbecoming for good order and military discipline" i.e. too much rum!

Coat of Arms above entrance to the Main Guard

This George III Coat of Arms is unique and was designed especially for this building. It is made of Coade Stone, that is not a stone but a ceramic made to resemble stone. The formula was invented by a Mrs. Eleanor Coade in 1779 and its foremost property is its durability. This example is dated 1803, faces directly into the prevailing weather and has withstood at least three major hurricanes. Both Kings George III and IV were enthusiastic about Coade Stone and their patronage of Mrs.Coade produced many important Crown and Governmental Commissions in the Americas and West Indies. Maybe this example was commissioned by King George III.

The Barbados Yacht Club, or Shot Hall as it was known, was erected in the British Garrison in 1810. It was the private residence of the Officer Commanding the Royal Engineers.
Collection of The Barbados Museum & Historical Society

Race Day, Savannah of St. Ann's, 1846 by W. S. Hedges
From the Collection of Barbados Museum & Historical Society

"St. Ann's Garrison and the Savannah -
Looking towards the Line Barracks, 1853"
By W. H. Freeman Lithographer E. Walker
Inspection of Troops on Savannah of St. Ann's
From the Collection of Barbados Museum & Historical Society

A cricket match on the Savannah circa 1870
Painting Kathleen C. Hawkins

This aerial photograph captures the complete Garrison Historic area. Charles Fort is in the top right hand corner and the other buildings can be traced from there. The Savannah was used by the British Troops for both drill and sports. Many of the main sports played today in Barbados such as cricket, football, athletics, horse racing, polo and boxing were all introduced during this period. The Annual Anniversary Parade celebrating Independence is also held on the Savannah.
Photo Felix Kerr

CHAPTER SEVEN

HISTORY OF THE
2nd WEST INDIA REGIMENT
1793 - 1920

In 1789 the French Revolution took place and was followed by war with Britain in 1793. The British were very short of soldiers owing to other commitments world wide. In 1795 the British Government approved the recruitment of slaves and two regiments, known as the West India Regiments, were raised with a compliment of one thousand men each. On enlistment the slaves automatically became Freed Men and were equipped and paid as British soldiers. By 1800 twelve regiments had been raised, a formidable fighting force. The 2nd West India Regiment was formed in Barbados and throughout the years recruited mainly from there. For this reason the regiment should be included in the Military History of Barbados and interesting details from some of the other regiments have also been included. They first saw action in the Carib War in St. Vincent in 1786 as the St. Vincent Rangers and then in the recapture of the islands from the French during the Napoleonic Wars. In 1815, after the Battle of Waterloo and defeat of the French, the regiments were reduced to two, the First and the Second. Throughout the 20th century one regiment kept the peace in the Caribbean, with its vast distances stretching from Guyana over to Belize and the other fought in West Africa

in the many campaigns there. In 1819 the 2nd Regiment was the first to be sent to West Africa to assist the British Army. Throughout the 19th century the 2nd Regiment was involved in the many punitive wars and expeditions. I have listed some of these as their exploits should not be forgotten. They are as follows:

The First Ashanti War 1823/24
The Cage Coote Expedition 1849
The Badiboo War 1860
The Quiah War 1861/62
The 2nd Ashanti War 1862/63
The Pram Pram Expedition 1867
The Gambia Expedition 1892
The Ashanti Expedition 1895/96

The above were not isolated skirmishes but full blooded wars and casualties were suffered on both sides. Two Victoria Crosses were awarded to men of the West India Regiments; one to Pte. Samuel Hodge of the 4th Regiment in 1868 and the other to Sgt. W. J. Gordon of the 1st in 1892. The 2nd Regiment saw action during World War One in East and West Africa and in Palestine. In 1920 the 2nd Regiment was absorbed into the 1st and the 1st themselves were disbanded in 1927. The Colours of the 1st were handed over to King George V and now hang in Windsor Castle. (See page 43).

Officer inspecting a guard of members of the 2nd West India Regiment
Author's collection

Uniforms of the West India Regiments
The 2nd W.I.R. is 4th from the left.
Artwork R. J. Marion for Military Modelling

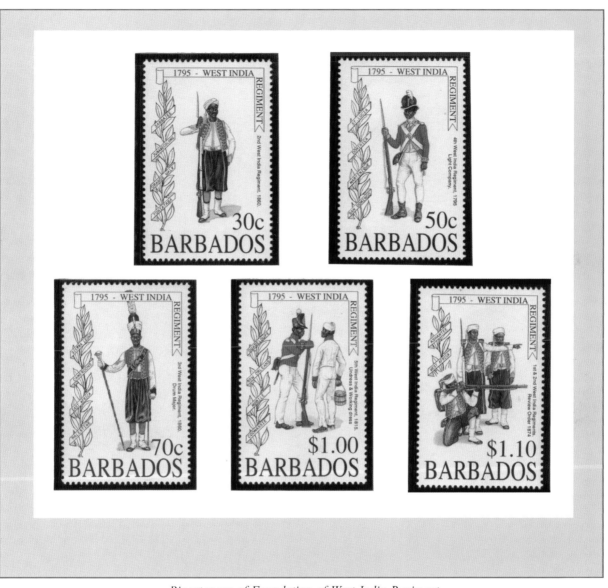

Bicentenary of Foundation of West India Regiment

1995, 21st February

30¢ Private, 2nd West India Regiment, 1860
50¢ Light Company Private, 4th West India Regiment, 1795
70¢ Drum Major, 3rd West India Regiment, 1860
$1.00 Privates in undress and working dress, 5th West India Regiment, 1815
$1.10 Troops from 1st and 2nd West India Regiments in Review Order, 1874

Barbados Philatelic Bureau, artwork by Don Cribbs

It was an engagement such as this in the Gambia at Tubabolong in West Africa that Private Hodges of 4th WIR was awarded the Victoria Cross for bravery
Author's collection

The Battle of Toniataba 1892. Sergeant W. Gordon 1st WIR was awarded the Victoria Cross after this battle.
Author's collection

Presentation of Ashantee Medals to the 2nd WIR on the Garrison Savannah in Barbados,

October 16th, 1875
Author's collection

WIR disembarking in West Africa
Author's collection

Gold Coast—Cape Coast Castle—"A" & "B" Companies of 2nd Battalion, West India Regiment

These two photographs show the 2nd West India Regiment on parade at Cape Coast Castle, Gold Coast. The one above refers to the 2nd Battalion, WIR and the other to the 2nd WIR. The renaming of the regiment into battalions took place in 1878 and therefore dates the photo
Barbados National Archives

2ND WEST INDIA REGIMENT ON PARADE AT CAPE COAST CASTLE.

Members of the 2nd West India Regiment at St. Ann's Fort, Barbados Circa 1895
Barbados National Archives

The Governor General inspecting a Guard of Honour from the 2nd West India Regiment
prior to their departure from Freetown, Sierra Leone for Barbados, late 19th century
Author's collection

The 1st West India Regiment on parade at St. Ann's Fort, Barbados circa 1890s

40

The 2nd West India Regiment on St. Ann's, Barbados circa 1880 Barbados National Archives

PRIVATES OF THE SECOND WEST INDIA REGIMENT

The Queen's Jubilee, June 26th 1897 (The Graphic)
Privates of the 2nd West India Regiment attending a Thanksgiving Day Service at St. Paul's Cathedral, London in 1897 to commemorate the completion of sixty years of Queen Victoria's reign.

The 2nd West India Regiment's detachment at Queen Victoria's Jubilee 1897
Barbados National Archives

41

The wearing of the Zouave uniform by the West India Regiments was sanctioned by Queen Victoria in 1858. She apparently had admired this uniform worn by the Zouave Algerian tribe which had been incorporated into the French Army. On the disbandment of the West India Regiments in 1927 the band of the Barbados Volunteer Force retained the uniform which is still worn by the Barbados Defence Force Band today.

Copy of original pen, ink & water colour drawing circa 1858, when change over from British Army uniform to the Zouave uniform was sanctioned by HM the Queen
Author's collection

The Colours of the West Indian Regiment that now hang in Windsor Castle
The Royal Collection © 2006, Her Majesty Queen Elizabeth 11

<u>OFFICERS, NON-COMMISSIONED OFFICERS AND MEN</u>

<u>OF THE WEST INDIA REGIMENT.</u>

    To me it is a sad task to bid farewell to a Regiment whose fine record of gallantry in the most arduous warfare covers nearly 150 years.

    Your Regimental Colours show distinguished service in the West Indies and West Africa, and I am glad to think that your achievements during the Great War in East Africa, Palestine and the Cameroons will be emblazoned on my Colour, and handed down to posterity.

    The West India Regiment has stood every test in peace and in war, thus earning an honoured name in the annals of the British Army. I am proud to take charge of your Colours, to be preserved and held in reverence as the outward and visible memorial of a famous Regiment.

    I gratefully thank all ranks for their loyal and devoted services to the Empire.

George R.I

18th February, 1927.

CHAPTER EIGHT

SLAVE REVOLT - DISBANDMENT OF MILITIA - BRITISH GARRISON - SIGNAL STATIONS 1815 - 1905

The Barbados Militia continued after the end of the Napoleonic Wars in 1815. At that time it is reported that there were six Regiments of Foot and a Troop of Life Guards (the Governor's Bodyguard). In 1869 the Militia and Yeomanry were disbanded. It may be that as a British Regiment was always on hand, the Government thought that the Militia was superfluous or their proposal to raise a Militia Tax was unacceptable to the Militias. For whatever reason they were disbanded and the Militia was not to emerge again until 1902 when the Barbados Volunteer Force was formed.

THE SLAVE REVOLT

On Sunday 14th April 1816 a slave revolt broke out in the parish of St. Philip in Barbados. Since it entailed a military response it should be studied here from a military point of view. The revolt took place against a background of the pending emancipation of the slaves and rumours circulating that their owners were trying to prevent their right to freedom. Slave rebellions in other nearby Caribbean Islands had met with some success, notably in Grenada and St. Vincent and of course in Haiti in which the French military had been forced to withdraw. However these islands, compared to Barbados, were mountainous and covered with forests and jungle and afforded a natural terrain in which to wage guerilla warfare, a type of warfare that European soldiers had not had any experience. However Barbados was totally different. There were no mountains or forests in which to hide and train. They would also be fighting a type of warfare that British trained troops, after the Napoleonic Wars, were probably the finest anywhere.

In planning a revolt such as this, a military person would have made an "Appreciation of the Situation". We would assume that Bussa, the leader of the coup, although only a slave, would have weighed his chances of success or have been advised by someone more cognizant than him as to his chances. His thought process would have run along the following lines.

FIRST, HIS AIM:

He was quite clear on this; the elimination of the slave owners and settlers and the seizure of power by the slaves.

SECOND, FACTORS FOR AND AGAINST HIM:

FOR:

At that time there were some 77,000 slaves in Barbados. If all were to rise up at the same time it would give him a substantial numerical advantage over his enemy. Given surprise, this advantage could win the battle for him.

AGAINST:

There were some 14,000 white settlers, who formed the basis of a very strong militia (part time soldiers) together with two regular British Regiments. All were well armed and trained. Bussa had no arms except the implements used for cutting cane. His communications to coordinate an island wide revolt were very limited.

THIRD, HIS DECISION:

Having weighed the factors he then had to make a decision. He must have realized that the success of the revolt relied on two factors. First, that upon hearing of his success in St. Philip the slave population in Barbados would rise as one. Secondly, he had to achieve surprise. He certainly achieved surprise but unfortunately the response by the slaves throughout the island was sporadic and hearing of Bussa's defeat, it petered out. Despite his bravery and that of his followers the result was disastrous for him. However emancipation was achieved a few years later and today he is numbered amongst the National heroes of Barbados. One is reminded of the remark by a French General whilst watching the Charge of the Light Brigade against the Russian guns. " C'est magnifique, mais ce n'est pas la guerre". (It's magnificent but it isn't war).

The Emancipation
Statue, St. Michael
Photo Felix Kerr

1st Viscount Combermere 1773 - 1865
in the uniform of Colonel of the 1st Life Guards c 1829
Painting by John Hayter ©
Collection of Victoria and Albert Museum, London

SIGNAL STATIONS

In 1817 Lord Combermere was appointed as Governor. He had had a distinguished military career. He soon recognized the necessity for a fast signals service to pass information around the island. He proposed setting up a series of signal stations at strategic places all over the countryside, which were in visual contact with each other. Before the stations were built there was a delay in notifying those who lived in the countryside of the arrival of ships with goods or mail. The local Government paid for the land and buildings and for their upkeep and the British Military supplied men to operate them. Flags and semaphore were the means of passing information. By 1819 a chain of five signal stations was completed in the interior of the country.

These Signal Stations were at:
Gun Hill, St. George
Montcrieffe, St. Philip
Cotton Tower, St. Joseph
Grenade Hall, St. Peter
Dover Fort, St. Peter

A further six were in the Bridgetown area
at strategic places such as:
Queens House (C in C Headquarters),
Central Police Station,
Charles Fort (Military),
Government Hall ,
Commercial House
Highgate.

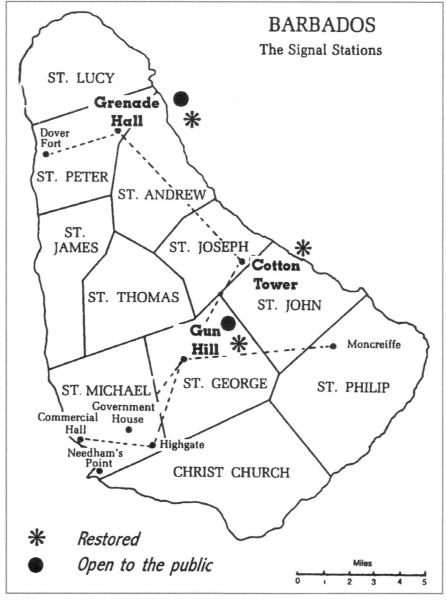

The Signal Station at Charles Fort to the left of the lighthouse, destroyed later by lightening

In 1883 the telephone was introduced into Barbados and the signal stations were closed and fell into disrepair. Thanks to the Barbados National Trust, Gun Hill and the Cotton Tower have been restored, as has Grenade Hall through private funding. During the rainy season many British regiments moved from the Garrison to Gun Hill because of the prevalence of mosquitoes and yellow fever in the Garrison. Whilst there in 1862 the Royal Scots Fusiliers built a road to the top of the hill which was and still is named Fusilier Road. On 30th of January 1988 HRH The Princess Margaret, Honorary Colonel in Chief of the Fusiliers, officially re-opened the road. The lion at the entrance to Fusilier Road was sculptured in 1868 by a Captain Henry Wilkinson of the 9th Regiment of Foot.

*Gun Hill
Signal Station
and the Lion
Postcard Collins
1910*

*HRH The Princess Margaret
opening Fusilier Road in 1988.
Gun Hill Signal Station in
the background
Photo Paul Foster Collection*

Infantry Camp at Gun Hill, late 19th Century
Photo Cooper, Warren Alleyne Collection

Military exercise, St. Ann's Garrison, Barbados, 1886
Unknown watercolour from the collection of the Barbados Museum & Historical Society

50

THE DAUNTLESS MEMORIAL

On the 15th of November 1852 Her Majesty's Screw Frigate "Dauntless", 33 guns, anchored in Carlisle Bay with Yellow Fever on board. She was not permitted to land. However all was done to assist those on board, but the fever took a heavy toll. Of a total compliment of 330 officers and men, 85 succumbed to the disease. A tomb was erected in St. Matthias Church as a memorial to those that died.

The Dauntless Memorial,
St. Matthias Churchyard
Photos Felix Kerr

Horse Racing at the Garrison

Up to 1906 horse racing was organized by the Military. The following photos by Cooper are dated 1891. They are from the author's private collection

A military band at a Race Meeting July 1891

Mr. Watts's horse 'Dagmar' and his jockey

'Blazeaway'

Inside the Paddock, Barbados Race Meeting, July 1891

Judges' Box, Barbados Race Meeting, July 1891

54

Barbados Race Meeting, July 1891

A game of cricket on the Savannah - 18 / 9 R.A.

The Main Guard, St. Ann's, Barbados. Note the clock on this side has only the hour hand

*St. Ann's
Garrison,
Barbados.
View from
Gun Site*

*Stone Barracks and West India barracks.
View from Main Guard*

57

*Garrison
St. Ann's
Barbados.
View from
Charles Fort
looking toward
St. Ann's Fort*

*This photograph shows the departure of the British troops
from the Engineers' pier in the Garrison in the early 20th
century. The last regiment to leave was the 4th Battalion
of the Worcestershire Regiment ending a hundred and
twenty-five years of British military presence in Barbados*
Warren Alleyne Collection

These four water colours of the Garrison, two on this page and two overleaf, are dated circa 1839, painted by soldier artists in the British Army, among whom were Arthur Pigott and C. M. Wilson. These were presented to the George Washington Museum in 2006 by the author and are displayed here by kind permission of the George Washington Museum.

View of Main Guard and Carlisle Bay

View of Garrison from Gun Site

59

View of Main Guard from Stone Barracks

View of Carlisle Bay
from Stone Barracks

CHAPTER NINE

BARBADOS VOLUNTEER FORCE - WW1 - WIRELESS STATION - ROLL OF HONOUR 1902 - 1939

The Barbados Volunteer Force (BVF) came into being on 2nd July 1902. It consisted of one infantry company of 50 members, one detachment of artillery and a detachment of cyclists. The Governor at the time was Sir Frederick Hodgson who became the first Commanding Officer. The last British Regiment was withdrawn in 1905 and the BVF would have taken over the responsibilities of Defence, Assistance to the Civil Power and Ceremonial. At a camp at Long Bay in 1909 a photo shows a total of approximately 120 all ranks. In 1911 a detachment of 2 officers and 8 sergeants represented the Force at the Coronation of King George V.

Sir Frederick Hodgson, KCMG. Governor of Barbados and Commanding Officer of the Barbados Volunteer Force, with a group of Officers at Long Bay Castle, St. Philip, 1902
Barbados National Archives

Major G. Lingwood,
Commanding Officer,
the Barbados Volunteer
Force, with a group of
Officers, circa 1904
Barbados National Archives

Major G. Lingwood, Commanding Officer,
the Barbados Volunteer Force
with a group of Officers, circa 1905.
Note the 9 pounder artillery guns.
Barbados National Archives

Officers Barbados Volunteers 1909-10
Standing: Lt. Reid, Lt. Walton, Lt. Haynes, Lt. Delamere, Lt. Evelyn,
Qm. Lt. Inniss, Lt. Simmons   Seated: Capt. Reece, Capt. Howell,
Chaplain Murray, Lt-Col F. J. Clarke, C.M.G Major The Hon. Capt. Wright,
Capt. Thorne, Lt. Cave
Barbados National Archives

1909/1910 Second
Camp Long Bay -
Church Parade
Barbados National Archives

The Coronation Contingent of the Barbados Volunteer Force before their departure for Britain in June 1911.
From left: Capt. S. C. Thorne, Lieut. J. R. Cave, Sergeants W. P. Bovell, A. G. Hinkson, R. B. Weatherhead,
J. Gibbons, H. C. Weatherhead, A. Fitzpatrick, J. Greaves, Lce.Sgt. A. D'V. Chase
Barbados National Archives

The departure of the Coronation Contingent of the Barbados Volunteer Force from Bridgetown to attend the
coronation of King George V on 22 June 1911
Barbados National Archives

Barbados Volunteer Force circa 1912
Barbados National Archives

BVF just before 1st World War
Barbados National Archives

THE FIRST WORLD WAR (WW1)
1914 - 1918

GV RI

HE whom this scroll commemorates was numbered among those who, at the call of King and Country, left all that was dear to them, endured hardness, faced danger, and finally passed out of the sight of men by the path of duty and self-sacrifice, giving up their own lives that others might live in freedom.

Let those who come after see to it that his name be not forgotten.

2/Lieut. Clement Forte Cave
103th Sqdn. Royal Air Force.

*Presented to the Military Museum
by the family of Clement Forte Cave*

During the War many Barbadians volunteered for service with the British and Canadian military abroad. Many of these were from the BVF. In 1925 a Cenotaph was erected in what is now Heroes Square and the names of all those Barbadians who gave their lives in the war were unveiled. Since then every year on Remembrance Day Parade these men are remembered in a solemn Memorial Service.

897

Vol. LIV

No. 58,

The Official Gazette.

EXTRAORDINARY

PUBLISHED BY AUTHORITY.

BRIDGETOWN, BARBADOS, 30th JUNE, 1919.

NOTICE.

With reference to the Government Notice of the 28th June 1919, the Public is informed the Salute of 101 guns ordered by His Majesty the King in honour of Peace having been signed by Germany will take place this afternoon, on the Savannah at 5 p.m., weather permitting.

By Command,

W. L. C. PHILLIPS,

Acting Colonial Secretary.

Colonial Secretary's Office,

30th June 1919.

Notice that there would be a Salute of 101 guns to celebrate Peace at the end of the First World War

The family of every soldier killed in the First World War received a Commemorative Brass Plaque and letter signed by King George V

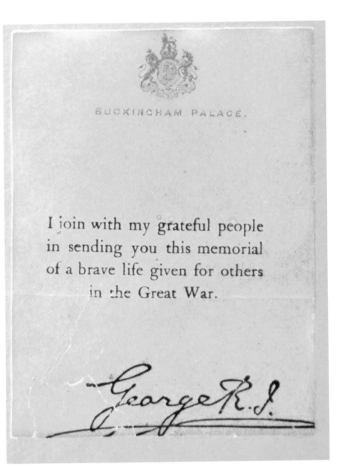

BUCKINGHAM PALACE.

I join with my grateful people in sending you this memorial of a brave life given for others in the Great War.

George R.I.

This plaque and the letter were presented to the Military Museum by the family of Hampden Trevor Ashby Cox

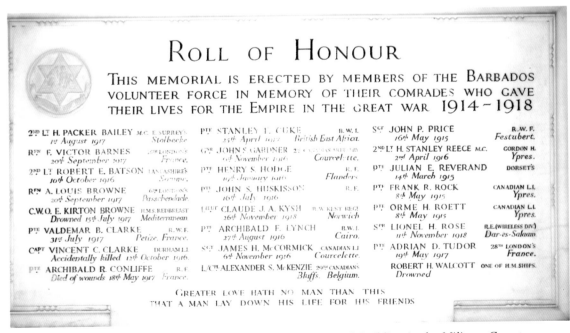

ROLL OF HONOUR

THIS MEMORIAL IS ERECTED BY MEMBERS OF THE BARBADOS VOLUNTEER FORCE IN MEMORY OF THEIR COMRADES WHO GAVE THEIR LIVES FOR THE EMPIRE IN THE GREAT WAR 1914~1918

2ND LT H. PACKER BAILEY M.C. E. SURREYS 1st August 1917 Stoibecke	PTE STANLEY L. COKE B.W.I. 25th April 1917 British East Africa	SGT JOHN P. PRICE R.W.F. 16th May 1915 Festubert.
RFN F. VICTOR BARNES 25th LONDON'S 20th September 1917 France.	GNR JOHN S. GARDNER 2nd CANADIAN ARTILLERY 6th November 1916 Courcelette.	2ND LT H. STANLEY REECE M.C. GORDON H. 2nd April 1916 Ypres.
2ND LT ROBERT E. BATSON LANCASHIRE'S 10th October 1916 Somme.	PTE HENRY S. HODGE R.F. 16th January 1916 Flanders	PTE JULIAN E. REVERAND DORSET'S 14th March 1915
RFN A. LOUIS BROWNE 6th LONDON'S 20th September 1917 Passchendaele.	PTE JOHN S. HUSKISSON R.F. 16th July 1916	PTE FRANK R. ROCK CANADIAN L.I. 8th May 1915 Ypres.
C.W.O. E. KIRTON BROWNE H.M.S. REDBREAST Drowned 15th July 1917 Mediterranean	LIEUT CLAUDE J. A. KYSH R.W. KENT REGT 26th November 1918 Norwich	PTE ORME H. ROETT CANADIAN L.I. 8th May 1915 Ypres.
PTE VALDEMAR B. CLARKE R.W.F. 31st July 1917 Petize. France.	PTE ARCHIBALD F. LYNCH B.W.I. 27th August 1916 Cairo.	STR LIONEL H. ROSE R.E. (WIRELESS DIV) 11th November 1918 Dar-es-Salaam
CAPT VINCENT C. CLARKE DURHAM L.I. Accidentally killed 12th October 1916.	SGT JAMES H. McCORMICK CANADIAN L.I 6th November 1916 Courcelette	PTE ADRIAN D. TUDOR 28TH LONDON'S 19th May 1917 France.
PTE ARCHIBALD R. CONLIFFE R.F. Died of wounds 18th May 1917 France.	L/CPL ALEXANDER S. McKENZIE 29TH CANADIANS Bluffs. Belgium.	ROBERT H. WALCOTT ONE OF H.M. SHIPS. Drowned

GREATER LOVE HATH NO MAN THAN THIS
THAT A MAN LAY DOWN HIS LIFE FOR HIS FRIENDS

Barbados Volunteer Force Roll of Honour in the Memorial Building in the Military Cemetery

Back Row: Capt. J. Connell, Capt. C. A. Brown, Lieut. H. A. Thorne, Lieut. B. Austin, Capt. E. A. Chase, Capt. E. L. Delamere, V.D., Lieut. F. C. Walcott, Lieut. A. H. S. Cox.

Sitting: Capt. J. E. Griffith, Capt. A. G. Kinch, Capt. F. B. Armstrong, Major J. R. M. Cave, O.B.E., V.D., Major A. De V. Chase, E.D., Major A. C. Thomas, Capt. C. A. Durant, Capt. C. R. Armstrong, Capt. H. H. Williams.

Front Row: 2nd Lieut. H. F. Alkins, Lieut. E. L. Sealy, 2nd Lieut. P. Mac D. Crichlow.

Absent: Capt. G. B. Evelyn, V.D., 2nd Lieut. S. O'C. Gittens.

Barbados National Archives

*BVF under command
of Lt-Col Wilkins,
OBE, MC before
WW2*
*Barbados National
Archives*

*Group of BVF
Officers late
1930s*
*Barbados National
Archives*

THE BRITISH WEST INDIES REGIMENT

Also during the war a regiment called the British West Indies Regiment was raised from volunteers all over the Caribbean, including Barbados, and saw service in France, Italy and the Middle East. This regiment was disbanded at the end of the war.

Badge of the British West Indies Regiment
Many Barbadians served with this Regiment

Officers BWI Regiment, Taranto, Italy c. 1918-1919
L to R Back: Capt. W. W. Morton, 2nd Lt. A. T. MacDonald,
Capt. Rev. R.A. Hendy, Lt. C. K. Smith, 2nd Lt. L. A. Chase,
2nd Lt. H. Austin Cooper, Capt. Rev. Father O'Brian
Centre: Capt. R. A. Hoban, Capt. A. S. Arrindell,
Maj. M. H. Smith, Lt. Col. A. de Boissiere, Capt. J. C. McLelland,
Capt. R. H. MacMinn, Capt. J. Niblock
Front: Lt. R. B. Skeete, Lt. H. W. Ince, Lt. C. R. Massey,
2nd Lt. H. C. Manning
Barbados National Archives

THE BARBADOS WIRELESS STATION

In 1914, at the outbreak of WW1, Barbados had no wireless communication with the outside world. Some enthusiastic amateurs from the BVF decided to erect one. Major Burdon and L/Cpl. Rose initially recruited Sgt. E.L. Armstrong, Cpl. L. A. Chase and Privates T.G. Layne, D.L. Chase and R.B. Armstrong to make up their team. By dint of borrowing and begging, often from passing ships, they erected the masts and station in St. Ann's Fort. Initially the distances both transmitting and receiving were small but by the end of WW1 the station could transmit up to 220 miles and could receive up to 400 miles, a remarkable achievement, which meant other islands and ships at sea could be contacted.

Between WW1 and WW2 the BVF continued with its usual training and ceremonial and aid to the civil powers. In 1939 at the start of WW2 it was embodied as the Barbados Battalion of the South Caribbean Forces (SCF).

This photograph shows the actual wireless set which was used to transmit and receive messages in World War One
Author's collection

The above photographs show the construction of the wireless mast on the side of the tower in St. Ann's Fort. Another mast of equivalent height was raised in the vicinity of the Stone Barracks
Author's collection

CHAPTER TEN

BARBADOS CADET CORPS
1904

Combermere: No. 3 Company,
Cadet Corps circa 1910
PhotoCadet Headquarters

The Barbados Cadet Corps was formed in 1904 with three school companies: Harrison College (No. 1), Lodge School (No.2) and Combermere (No. 3). These companies were formed by masters who had previously joined the Barbados Volunteer Force (BVF). However it was not until 1909 that these companies became officially affiliated to the BVF. In 1978 Ellerslie School became the fourth unit to join the Corps. In 1981 Government decided that all secondary schools should be incorporated into the Corps. At present there are a total of 24 units, which include 21 at schools, 1 independent unit, the Sea Scouts unit and the Cadet Corps Band as a separate unit. Cadet Headquarters is located in Cherry Cottage on the Savannah. There are a total of 60 officers and 1,400 cadets and it is hoped to raise this number to 5,000 cadets by the year 2010. Girls were introduced into the Corps in 1974 and there is a ratio of approximately 2 to 1 in favour of the boys.

1914

Lodge: No. 2 Company,
Cadet Corps circa 1910
O.C. Capt. R. R. Hall
(1903 - 1914)
Photo Cadet Headquarters

2004

Sea Scouts in 2004
Photo Cadet Headquarters

Cadet Corps Band in 2006
Photo Cadet Headquarters

CHAPTER ELEVEN

WW2 - BARBADOS BATTALION OF THE SOUTH CARIBBEAN FORCES
BARBADOS HOME GUARD
VOLUNTEERS FOR SERVICE OVERSEAS
1st CARIBBEAN REGIMENT
SINKING OF THE CORNWALLIS
1939 - 1945

Bren Group from the Barbados
Battalion of the South
Caribbean Forces
practicing drills during WW2
Barbados National Archives

THE BARBADOS BATTALION OF THE SOUTH CARIBBEAN FORCES

Soon after the outbreak of WW2 the Barbados Volunteer Force was mobilized and became the Barbados Battalion of the South Caribbean Forces, whose headquarters was in Trinidad. Its role was the defence of Barbados in case of enemy attack. It was organized as a standard infantry battalion with four rifle companies and a headquarters company. Lieut.-Colonel Wilkins who had been Commanding Officer of the BVF had taken over the command of the Battalion.

*Soldiers of the
Barbados Battalion
of the South
Caribbean Forces
on exercise in 1942
during World War II*
Barbados National Archives

*The Barbados
Battalion of the South
Caribbean Forces
on training exercise in
1943. The winning
team of the Inter-Rifle
Shooting Competition*
Barbados National Archives

Back Row, L. to R.   Lt. P. E. Johnson, Lt. A. S. Warren, Lt. F. N. Grannum, *M.O. B.V.F. Attached.* Lt. C. N. P. Weatherhead,
Lt. J. D. Alleyne, *R.A.M.C.* Lt. G. F. Austin, Lt. H. A. Dowding, Lt. G. L. N. Parker.
Middle Row: Capt. L. Lipsham, Capt. B. W. G. Austin, Capt. H. E. Skeete, *M.O. B.V.F. Attached.* Major W. Gibbens, *2nd I/C.*
Lt.-Col. H. Wilkin, *O.B.E., M.C.,C.O.* Capt. H. H. Lee, *Adjt.* Capt. J. E. Griffith, Capt. F. M. Dowlen, *Chaplain.*
Capt. O. F. C. Walcott, Capt. M. B. Hutt.
Front Row: 2/Lt. L. C. Banfield, 2/Lt. F. K. N. Mascoll, 2/Lt. L. A. Chase, 2/Lt. J. Redhead.
Absent on duty: Capt. E. L. Sealy, Lt. R. A. Sealy, Lt. M. M. Seale, Lt. L. A. Williams.

South Caribbean Forces - 1st April 1943
Barbados National Archives

The King's Birthday Parade, St. Michael, 1943 The Governor of Barbados,
Sir Hillary Blunt, takes the Salute of the Barbados Battalion of the South Caribbean Forces
Barbados National Archives

THE BARBADOS HOME GUARD

The Barbados Home Guard was formed in 1943. The object of this unit was to augment the defences of the island by providing local defence and protection of vulnerable points. They were unpaid and operated out of their homes and only at night. They were divided into platoons of 2 officers, 1 sergeant and 30 other ranks. They were armed with submachine guns and rifles and wore uniform when on duty. Major J.O. Connell, later Colonel, was the Commandant of the Force.

The Barbados Home Guard, 1943,
Lt. Roberts
Barbados National Archives

The Barbados Home Guard 1943
The King's Birthday Parade on the Savannah.
The Governor of Barbados, Sir Hillary Blunt takes the Salute
Barbados National Archives

VOLUNTEERS FOR SERVICE OVERSEAS

ATS Contingent in the Victory March
Past in London in 1945
Photo: Margaret Walcott

Soon after the outbreak of World War Two (WW2) many Barbadian men and women volunteered to fight in the armed services of both Britain and Canada. In those days it was a fairly expensive and risky exercise to get to either of these countries. In order to pay for their passages by ship and general expenses, a fund was set up to which the general public and businesses were asked to contribute. A Mr. Wright even funded his own contingent. The Volunteers fought with British and Canadian forces all over the world, many did not return and their names are on the Cenotaph in Heroes Square. Also volunteering for service abroad were many women who went to join the war effort in both Britain and Canada. Many of them left Barbados in September 1943 by ship for Trinidad where they met up with other contingents of women from other islands. They went in a convoy of ships first to New York and then across the Atlantic to Britain. Many of them trained at the Auxiliary Training Service (ATS) depot and then were posted to various units throughout the UK. They were there to celebrate the end of hostilities in Europe and Japan and took part with the ATS contingent in the Victory March through London.

Muriel Jackman, ATS, a volunteer from Barbados

A group of women volunteers from the Caribbean in training with the Auxiliary Training Service in U.K.
Photo: Margaret Walcott

*Mr. Wright's Contingent - The First Barbados Contingent of Volunteers for the
Armed Forces which sailed from Barbados on July 27, 1940*

BACK ROW (l. to r.) Colin Bowen, W. Ward, R. Ward, D. Ince. P. King, S. Edghill, B. Johnston.
FRONT ROW (l. to r.) Leon Foster, John Skinner, G. Marshall, Clyde Lewis, J. Manning, Willie
Foster, J. Rose.

*The First R.A.F. Recruits
- The Second Barbados
Contingent*

*Note Errol W. Barrow
in the back row
Photos The Christmas
Mirror, 1940*

BACK ROW (l. to r.)—C. P. King, J. S. Partridge, A. A. Walrond, J. L. L. Yearwood, M. R. Cuke,
E. W. Barrow.
FRONT ROW—G. D. Cumberbatch, A. P. C. Dunlop, H. E. S. Worme, G. A. Barrow, A. O. Weekes,
B. F. H. Miller.

82

Vice Admiral H. C. Bovell, Royal Navy

Admiral Bovell was the highest ranking Barbadian in any of the British Services in WW2. He was born in 1893 in Chelston and entered the Royal Navy in 1910. In World War Two he had reached the rank of Captain RN and was in command of the Aircraft Carrier "HMS Victorious". In 1941 in the North Sea the German Battleship "Bismark", which had been doing great damage to allied shipping, was located. Immediately Captain Bovell sent nine torpedo carrying Swordfish aircraft to attack the "Bismark". One of these torpedoes damaged its steering gear and immobilized the ship which was eventually sunk. He was awarded the CBE and later the DSO for bravery
(Photo Warren Alleyne Collection)

HMS Victorious 1941
Barbados Philatelic Bureau, 2003 -
Designer John Batchelor

Battleship RM Bismark
Photo © Blohm & Voss Shipyard, Hamburg

Flying Officer Errol Walter Barrow was one of many Barbadian Volunteers to serve with the British Services. He became a navigator in the Royal Air Force in Bomber Command. He completed thirty missions over Europe and in those days it was considered a miracle if you were still alive and you were excused any further flying duties. It was no wonder that with such devotion to duty he became the first Prime Minister of Barbados.
Margaret Walcott Collection

Barbadian Volunteers leaving the island for service in the UK during WWII
Barbados National Archives

*Flight Lieutenant Winston K. (Pony) Hynam,
Distinguished Flying Cross (DFC) and
Distinguished Flying Medal (DFM) was born
in Bridgetown in 1917. In the Second World
War he volunteered for service in the Royal
Air Force. He became a wireless operator
and a front gunner in a bomber squadron;
a position that was always in danger from
attacking enemy fighters. He flew a total of
fifty missions and lived to tell the tale which
in itself was a miracle. He received two
awards for bravery.
Penny Hynam Collection*

*Photographs of some of those
Barbadians who volunteered
for service abroad*

*Pilot A. Weekes
R.A.F*

*Sjt. Pilot M. R. Cuke
R.A.F.V.R. Killed in Action*

Pte. G. H. Nurse

Fl/Off. G. H. Inniss
R..A.F. Killed in Action

Pte. B. E. Boyce

G. D. Cumberbatch
R.A.F.V.R. Killed in Action

Pte. G. V. E. Forde

Noel Goddard, R.A.F.

Pte. W. E. Haynes

Fl/Off H. F. V. Smith
R.A.F.
Killed in Action

Pte. A. E. Marshall

Pte. E. Payne

Gnr. D.C. Barker

Pte. W.I. Holmes

P. King, RN

Pte. D.M. Watts

Pte. A. Bayley

Pte. Julian Byer

J.L.L. Yearwood, R.A.F.

Flt-Lt C.D. Ince,
DFC and Bar R.A.F.V.R.
Killed in Action

87

1ST CARIBBEAN REGIMENT

On 27th March 1944 the Barbados Contingent of the would be Caribbean Regiment embarked on the "*SS Corsair*", destination the United States. It was, however, to stop at practically every island to take on additional contingents. On arrival in the States it was sent to Fort Eustace where the Regiment completed six weeks of training and then on 1st July 1944 it embarked on the "*SS Santa Rosa*", destination unknown. Having passed by the Straits of Gibraltar into the Mediterranean they were told that their destination was Italy where they would experience their first taste of action. However they would have to complete more training to get acclimatized to the country. By the time they finished the German Army was in full retreat and they were no longer required. This was a disappointment for the men of the Regiment who had trained so hard and reckoned they were battle fit. This was substantiated later by General Allfrey who had sent a message to Field Marshall Alexander telling him that the Carib Regiment was ready for action. The reply came back "I am proud to receive the Carib Regiment". In October 1944 the Regiment embarked for Egypt and it was not until the end of 1945 that they embarked for home.

1st Reinforcement Company
Elvey Watson Collection

THE SINKING OF CNS CORNWALLIS

On the 11th of September 1942 at 4.30 pm the quiet daily life of Barbadians, in a war they had not seen or heard, was suddenly shattered by a series of explosions that reverberated around Bridgetown. Some thought that the enemy was attacking but the more curious, such as a young Warren Alleyne, ran down to Carlisle Bay. He was in time to see the Canadian National Steamship freighter, "*Cornwallis*", settling on the shallow sands of the Bay, its superstructure above water. It transpired that a German submarine had blown a hole in the protective underwater netting in the Bay and sunk the Cornwallis. However, the ship being in shallow water, was repaired and re-floated, only to be sunk again in the Atlantic. The German U-Boat 514 which was commanded by Lt.Commander Hans Jurgen Auffermann was itself sunk, with all hands, later in the war in 1943 by a Liberator aircraft of 224 Squadron RAF. Ironically this was Barbadian Derek Davies' squadron!

German U-Boat
Public Domain

Canadian National Steamship Freighter Cornwallis, sunk 11 September 1942
Photo by Capt. W.H.R. Armstrong - Warren Alleyne Collection

CHAPTER TWELVE

THE BARBADOS REGIMENT (BR)
1948 - 1979

*Regiment detachment to Coronation of
QE II, 1953 Lt. S.E. Lance Johnson, later
Capt., ED, Sgt. Hugh C. Hill, Capt., ED,
Sgt. Norton Reid, CSM George Carter*
Photo Ralph Johnson Collection

In 1947 the Barbados Battalion of the South Caribbean Forces was disbanded and Lt.-Colonel J. O. Connell was appointed by the Governor to reconstitute the Barbados Volunteer Force and re-designate it as the Barbados Regiment (BR). As a Regiment they were able to carry Colours and on 23rd February 1953 the Colours were duly presented to them by Princess Alice, The Princess Royal, who was gazetted Honorary Colonel of the Barbados Regiment in 1955.

Lt.-Colonel J. O. Connell became the first Commanding Officer and later became its Honorary Colonel. The Regiment carried out its normal duties as an Armed Reserve Unit. The first overseas camp was held in St. Vincent in 1961 and in St. Lucia in 1962 and 1963. Two hundred and fifty all ranks attended the camp in 1963. In 1974 female soldiers were recruited into the BR and the first one to sign up was Pte. Florence Gittens, now Lt.-Colonel F. E. Gittens. In 1979 the Barbados Defence Force (BDF) was formed and the Regiment became the reserve element of the Regular Force. Events after 1979 are included in the chapter dealing with the BDF.

Officers of the newly formed Barbados Regiment 1948

Standing L - R: 2/Capt. P. Peterkin, 2/Capt. T. Gittens, Capt. R. Daniel, Capt. L. Johnson, Capt. J. Redhead, Capt. R. Jordan, Capt. C. Neblett, Capt. L. Gittens, Capt. G. Goddard, Capt. W. Lashley, 2/Capt. Peterkin. Sitting L - R: Capt. G. Hunte, Capt.(Dr.) Grannum, Capt. Dowling (Padre), Major (Dr.) Skeete, UK Officer, Capt. J. Connell, Capt. A. Warren, Capt. C. Weatherhead, Capt. L. Chase, Capt. R. Perkins, Capt. V. McComie
Barbados National Archives

The unveiling on the Cenotaph of the names of those killed in World War Two during the Remembrance Day Service in November 1951
Barbados National Archives

Presentation of Colours by
HRH Princess Alice,
The Princess Royal,
23rd February 1953
2nd Lt. G. C. Peterkin,
Major C.E.P. Weatherhead,
H.R.H. The Princess Alice,
2nd Lt. L.G. Quintyne,
Major A.S. Warren,
Hon. R. N. Turner
Photo BR Collection

The completion of the Presentation of Colours
Photo BR Collection

*New Colours marching
off parade after
presentation in 1953
Photo BR Collection*

*HRH The Princess Alice departing from Seawell,
Guard Commander reporting
Photo BR collection*

March Past Queen's Birthday Parade
Photo BR Collection

Queen's Birthday parade 1965
Capt. A. Batson, Lt. J. Sealy
Photo BR Collection

94

Camp Walkers. 1956
Photo BR Collection

Officers of the Barbados Regiment 1960

Standing L-R: Lt. A. Batson, Lt. H. Blackman, Lt. L. Quintyne, Lt. T. Thorne, Lt. H. Hill, 2/Lt. J. Sealy, 2/Lt. C. Crane Sitting L-R: Major W. Browne, Major H. Dowding, Lt. Col. J. Connell, Major L. Banfield, Major R. Jordan, Major M. Hill
Photo BR Collection

Visit of HM the Queen,
late 1960s
Colonel J. O. Connell and
Lt. Colonel Walcott
in attendance
Photo BR Collection

Visit HRH The Princess Alice.
This was the first time she wore the
uniform as Honorary Colonel of the Regiment.
Colonel J. O. Connell in attendance.
Photo BR Collection

CHAPTER THIRTEEN

BARBADOS DEFENCE FORCE
FIRST 28 YEARS INCLUDING THE
BARBADOS COAST GUARD
1979 - 2007

On 15th August 1979 the Barbados Defence Force (BDF) came into being, the first all regular unit in the military history of Barbados. Many of the Barbados Regiment (BR) Reserves, both officers and other ranks, were given the option of joining full time or remaining on the reserve. Many of them took up the offer of a regular engagement. There was however not enough regular experienced Officers or NCOs to train a fledgling force and contract positions were advertised in Britain. At about the same time many Barbadians who had joined the British Services direct in the early sixties were completing their twenty two years' service with the Colours and were looking for something to do in their retirement. Many took up the offer of joining the BDF and their experience was invaluable.

HRH The Princess Margaret inspecting the Guard of Honour prior to her presenting new Colours to the Barbados Regiment in 1981. Colonel (Brigadier) R. E. C. Lewis, Major H. W. Blackman (Lt. Colonel) and Major C. Mapp were in attendance
Photo Felix Kerr

The Queen's Colour of The Barbados Regiment.

*The Queen's Colour of
The Barbados Regiment*

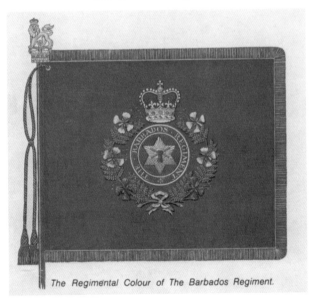

The Regimental Colour of The Barbados Regiment.

The Regimental Colour of the Barbados Regiment

The first ceremonial parades which the BDF took part in were the Remembrance Day Parade and Service and the Independence Parade at the end of November 1979. These parades have been held every year ever since. The re-dedication of the Military Cemetery took place in 1981 and the Presentation of New Colours to the BR by HRH The Princess Margaret was held in 1982. In October 1983 the BDF was part of a Caribbean Force which was involved with the U.S. Military in the rescue mission to Grenada (see Chapter 14). Meanwhile the BDF was involved in disaster relief throughout the Caribbean. Hurricanes in 1988, 1989, 1995 and 2004 struck Jamaica, Montserrat, St. Kitts, Antigua and Grenada. In 1999 Montserrat was devastated by a volcanic eruption and in 1994 the BDF was part of the United Nations Force keeping peace in Haiti.

By 1983 the Medical Reception Station (MRS) was completed, under the guidance of Lt.-Colonel F. E. Gittens, which also included accommodation for the women soldiers. A diving decompression chamber was installed in 1988 which not only gave relief to divers in trouble but was also used by civilian patients in the field of hyperbaric medicine. The MRS was also built as a back up to the Queen Elizabeth Hospital in case of an emergency and has its own trained medical staff and ambulance service.

Guards of Honour for Royalty and Heads of State were mounted on many occasions. Most notable of these were for HM The Queen when she opened the 350th Anniversary of Parliament in 1989 and the State Dinner which was held in the Officers' Mess of the BDF. Presidents Reagan and Clinton from the United States also visited. In 1984 a separate barracks was built at Paragon for the former Commando Squadron. It was sited next to the Grantley Adams Airport and having easy access to the ABC Highway could ensure quick response to any emergency. The first Chief of Staff in 1979 was Colonel L. C. Banfield to be followed by Colonel R.E.C. Lewis (later Brigadier) and then by Colonel A.E. Quintyne in 2002.

HRH The Princess Margaret presenting the New Colours to the Barbados Regiment.
Lt. (Major) V. Gittens and Lt. L. Moe received the Colours. Major (Lt. Col) L. Quintyne was
in attendance
Photo The Advocate

*The Rt. Hon. E. W. Barrow, Prime Minister takes
the salute at the march past of the Barbados
Regiment detachment in St. Ann's Fort in 1984
Lt. Col L. G. Quintyne is in attendance.
Lieut. J. Ward is shown on parade. The women
soldiers' detachment is in the background.*
Photo The Advocate

*The Rt. Hon. J.M.G.M. (Tom) Adams, Prime Minister takes
the salute at the annual parade of the Barbados Defence Force
in 1983. Brigadier R.E.C. Lewis is in attendance and on parade
is Captain (Lt. Colonel) W. Parris, Lieut. (Major) N. Brathwaite
and Lieut. O. Sinckler.*
Photo The Advocate

The Colours of the Barbados Regiment march past on an Independence Parade Colour Sergeant R. Graham and Colour Sergeant N. Williams
Photo Felix Kerr

Headquarters Squadron marches past H.E. The Governor General on the Independence Parade. Lt. (Major) N. Brathwaite and Colour Sergeant (Lt.) C. Belgrave are on parade
Photo Errol Nurse

*A typical crowd
scene at an
Independence
Parade held on
the Savannah,
30th November
every year
Photo Felix Kerr*

*The Guard of
Honour from the
Barbados Defence
Force
awaiting the arrival
of the
Governor-General
for the annual
opening of
Parliament*

*Her Majesty The Queen and the Duke of Edinburgh attending the State Dinner in the Officers' Mess of the
Barbados Defence Force in 1989. Previously The Queen had opened the 350th Anniversary of
the Sitting of Parliament, the second oldest in the Commonwealth after Westminster.
Others in the photograph include H.E. Sir Hugh Springer, Governor General and Lady Springer and
the Rt. Hon. Erskine Sandiford, Prime Minister and Mrs. Sandiford.
Photo Brooks La Touche*

HM The Queen receiving a Royal Salute from the Guard of Honour of the Barbados Defence Force at Grantley Adams Airport in 1989. Also in the reception line from left to right were Capt. N. Martindale, Brigadier R.E.C. Lewis, Capt (Lt-Col.) J. B. Bostick, HE Sir Hugh Springer, Governor General, Police Commissioner Mr. Orville Durant and the Rt. Hon. Erksine Sandiford, Prime Minister. Concorde aircraft in the background.
Photo The Nation

Instructing Staff at Harrison Point Camp 1981
L - R: Cpl. (Sgt.) E. Young, Cpl. (CSgt.) D.Craigwell,
Sgt. D. Waithe, Lt. (Maj.) S. B. Reece, Capt. (Maj.) C. Brathwaite, WO2 R.C. Beckles, Lt. (Capt.) W. Martindale,
Sgt. (WO2) V. Bovell, Cpl. (Sgt.) E. Bowen, Cpl. (WO2) H. B. Smith
Photo BDF Collection

The official opening of the Corporals' Mess St Ann's Fort
L-R: Cpl. (WO2) N. E. D. Williams, LCpl. (Lt. (CG)) B. Roberts, Col. R. Griffith, LCpl. (Sgt.) B. Worrell,
Cpl. C. Brewster, Cpl. (Sgt.) E. Branch, LCpl J. Williams, L S. (CPO) T. Peterson, LCpl. V. Holder,
LCpl. (WO2) Mc R. Jones, LCpl. (Sgt) J. Thompson, Cpl. R. Branch, Cpl. D. Nurse
Seated: Lt. Col. L. G. Quintyne, WO1 G. Johnson
Photo BDF Collection

The Band of the Barbados Defence Force in their Zouave Uniforms parading in front of Edinburgh Castle at the Edinburgh Tattoo in 1999. The Director of Music Lieut. R. Beckles is behind Drum Major H. B. Smith.

Trooping the Colour at the Bridgetown Port in 1988. The Bands of the Barbados Defence Force, the Royal Barbados Police Force, the Anglian Regiment and the Jamaica Military Band were all on parade.
Photo The Nation

The Cenotaph Guard in front of the Cenotaph in Heroes' Square.
The Remembrance Parade is held annually in November, in which those
Barbadians who gave their lives in the two world wars are remembered.
From L-R: RBPF Rep. Sgt. A. Lopez, WO2 C. Blenman,
Sgt. R. Blackman, Sgt. D. Morgan, PO R. Sealy
Photo Errol Nurse

President Reagan, President of the United States of America,
inspecting a Guard of Honour from the Barbados Defence Force
on his arrival at Grantley Adams Airport in 1988. Lt. Col. L. G. Quintyne is in attendance
Photo The Nation

His Excellency
Fetus Mogae,
President of Botswana,
on State Visit in 2004.
L-R: WO2 N. Williams,
Lieut. (CG) G. Anthony,
Major R. Vickers
Photo BDF Collection

Barbados Defence Force Guard of Honour and
Barbadian Legionnaires on Remembrance Day Parade
in Heroes Square, Bridgetown
Photo BDF Collection

In 1977 the original Coastguard (CG) base at Oistins was moved to Willoughby Fort in Bridgetown and became part of the Division of Defence and Security in the Prime Minister's Office. The CG came under the direct control of the Commanding Officer of the Barbados Regiment. When the Barbados Defence Force was formed in 1979 the CG became an integral part of the Force and was responsible directly to the Chief of Staff.

In order to meet its commitments, additional ships were acquired and on 20th October 1982 the Flagship "HMBS Trident" was commissioned. She had been built in England and the most senior coastguard officer on her maiden voyage was Lt.-Commander C. Emtage of the Reserve.

As with the Army, outside assistance was required to train the Officers and senior NCOs. This assistance was provided by the Royal Navy. Lieut.-Commander C. Belle was appointed the first Barbadian Officer Commanding the Coastguard. He has been succeeded over the years by Lt.-Cdr. W. Kirton (Commander), Lt.-Cdr. W. Lashley, Lt.-Cdr. D. Dowridge (Commander), Lt.-Cdr. K. Jones and Lt.-Cdr. R. Shurland in 2001.

The CG quickly found itself involved with disaster relief throughout the islands, taking men and materials to whichever island needed help. It has also supplied help to flood victims in Barbados itself on many occasions.

In 1979, on the day after the Maurice Bishop Coup in Grenada, "HMBS George Ferguson" entered St. George's Harbour under the guns on the fort and as Lieutenant-Commander P. Tomlin recalled, he wasn't quite sure what sort of reception he would get. In fact Bishop himself came aboard and agreed for some diplomatic personnel, who wished to leave Grenada, to go on board.

The Coastguard has been fully engaged in patrolling the maritime borders, search and rescue operations and the interdiction of drug smugglers using high speed boats between the islands. The base at Willoughby Fort has proved very vulnerable to high seas, particularly associated with hurricanes. A new and more protected base, north of The Deep Water Harbour and close to the existing Flour Mill, has been identified and the Coastguard move is scheduled to be completed by 2007.

The Coastguard aloft during the Grand Spectacular Tattoo held in November 1987
Photo BDF Collection

The Commissioning Ceremony for HMBS Willoughby Fort.
HMBS Trident in the background
Photo Errol Nurse

HMBS Willoughby Fort
Photo Errol Nurse

The Coastguard on Parade for the first time in 1979.
Their uniforms had not been issued.
Photo Errol Nurse

The Coastguard marching on to parade with their dress
uniforms and sub machine guns.
Photo Errol Nurse

HMBS Trident, flagship of the Fleet
Photo Errol Nurse

HMBS Enterprise
Photo Errol Nurse

HMBS Excellence
Photo Errol Nurse

HMBS George Ferguson
Photo Errol Nurse

The two ships shown here and HMBS Enterprise shown on previous page were decommissioned during the 1990s

OFFICERS COMMANDING THE COASTGUARD 1980 – 2004

Lt. Cdr. C. V. Belle

Lt. Cdr. W. N. Kirton

Lt. Cdr. W. Lashley

Lt. Cdr. D. A. Dowridge

Lt. Cdr. K. Jones

Lt.Cdr. R. Shurland

Coast Guard inflatable at speed
Photo Errol Nurse

CHAPTER FOURTEEN

OPERATION "URGENT FURY" THE RESCUE MISSION TO GRENADA 1983

On the 13th of November 1979 in the island of Grenada, 110 miles west of Barbados, a coup removed the existing elected government of Sir Eric Gairy and superimposed a dictatorship on the country. The leader of the Coup was Maurice Bishop and, with his deputy Bernard Coard, they installed themselves as Prime Minister and Deputy Prime Minister respectively. Soon after seizing power they established diplomatic relations with Libya, Cuba and an assortment of Communist Eastern European nations. In 1983 Maurice Bishop began to realize that Cuba and its Communist allies were going to use, and indeed were already using, Grenada as a launching pad to subvert the rest of the Caribbean islands. His deputy, realizing that he was wavering from the hardliners, ordered him to be put under house arrest. Hearing this, a crowd marched to Bishop's house, released him and took him into the town to speak to the people. Coard, seeing this, sent some armoured cars to disperse the crowd and dispose of Bishop. This they did. Bishop was killed and many of his supporters slaughtered. A curfew was imposed and Grenadians, not knowing what was going on, feared for their lives and their future. Meanwhile on 21st October 1983 there was a meeting of the Organization of Eastern Caribbean States (OECS) in Barbados. The decision was taken to ask the United States of America to take military action to fill the political vacuum in Grenada. It was also agreed that a Caribbean Force should accompany the Americans. President Reagan agreed to military action and had already diverted the 7th Fleet which was in the Atlantic. In the

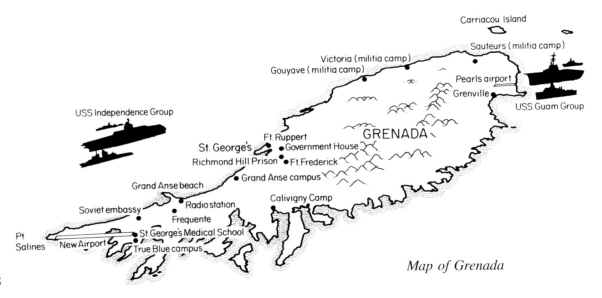

Map of Grenada

The Barbadian Contingent of the Caribbean Force about to embark in a C130 for Grenada.
On the left Brigadier R.E.C. Lewis, Commanding the Caribbean Force, and behind him is the author
Photo Errol Nurse

early hours of Tuesday 25th October 1983 the attack on Grenada was launched from Barbados. History once again repeated itself as in the past Barbados was always the launching pad for attacks on the islands. With such a massive force the assault was all over in a few days, much to the relief of the Grenadians. What was a real threat to the Caribbean was removed and Grenada returned to democratic government. To those of the Caribbean Force who saw the extent of the airport runway (ostensibly for tourists from undisclosed destinations) and the stockpile of military equipment, it became quite apparent exactly why Maurice Bishop had to be removed.

A dismantled Russian BRDM troop carrier
Photo Errol Nurse

A Russian 23mm twin
anti-aircraft gun beneath
24 Pdr cannon on the walls
of the fort
Photo Errol Nurse

The day after the coup
Maurice Bishop boards
HMBS George Ferguson in
St. George's Harbour
Photo Charles Hackett,
The Nation

Mrs. Phyllis Coard, wife of Bernard Coard, under arrest by members of the Caribbean Force
Photo Errol Nurse

Caribbean Force members guarding
Cuban prisoners who had been armed
and in control of the airport.
Photo Errol Nurse

IN MEMORY OF
THOSE SERVICEMEN OF THE
UNITED STATES OF AMERICA
WHO GAVE THEIR LIVES
DURING THE RESCUE OPERATION IN
GRENADA
25 OCTOBER 1983

Memorial in the Barbados
Military Cemetery to the
nineteen US servicemen
who lost their lives during
the rescue operation
Photo Felix Kerr

CHAPTER FIFTEEN
HIGH ALTITUDE RESEARCH PROJECT (HARP)
1962 - 1978

Although HARP was, and is, largely unknown it is historically, scientifically and militarily unique. It is for this reason that it should be included in a military history of Barbados.

Barbados was chosen as a launching site because of its proximity to the Atlantic Missile Range. In 1962 a 16" gun was moved to Barbados and was installed and test fired by January 1963. In 1965 the gun was extended by adding a second barrel to the first and considerably increasing the range. HARP's accomplishments remain a remarkable record. Some of these achievements are:

a. Set a new high altitude record for ballistic probes into space of 180 kilometers, unbeaten to this day.

b. Proved that artillery employing rocket boosters could sustain accurate fire for up to 250 miles.

c. Mapped and measured the ionospheric winds that so effect our weather patterns on earth.

d. Succeeded in delivering heavy payloads into space for a mere fraction of the cost of conventional rocketry.

After widespread publicity in the British, Canadian, American and Caribbean media that HARP was to perfect a long range artillery system for South Africa and Israel, the Barbadian Government closed the project down in 1978. The supporters of it maintained that the project was dedicated solely to the application of technology to gun launched systems for the purpose of non-military oriented altitude and space research. Whatever the final verdict, Barbados was left a unique modern gun to match the unique gun of the year 1600 to be seen in the National Armouries.

The extended HARP Gun firing at maximum elevation

A water colour by Aileen Hamilton showing the 16" gun being off loaded from the ship on to railway line for transportation to Paragon
Author's collection

HARP Gunsite Barbados
Extreme left: Prime Minister
Errol Barrow Third from left:
Lt.Gen. James Gavin,
US Army Fourth:
The Hon. Rolland Michener,
Governor General of Canada

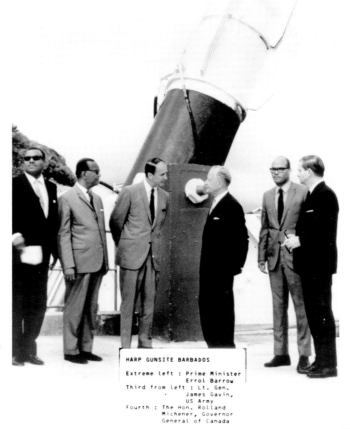

HARP GUNSITE BARBADOS

Extreme left : Prime Minister
Errol Barrow
Third from left : Lt. Gen.
James Gavin,
US Army
Fourth : The Hon. Rolland
Michener, Governor
General of Canada

CHAPTER SIXTEEN
THE NATIONAL ARMOURY

All through the 17th, 18th and 19th centuries Britain supplied Barbados with guns (cannon). It was very important to Britain from the early 17th century that Barbados should be heavily defended. A succession of forts and gun emplacements were built along the south and west coasts. Because of the reefs down the east coast no forts were necessary.

A survey completed in 1780 lists 40 forts or gun employments and 364 guns within the space of 30 miles. Most of these guns were made of iron and when they became obsolete their wooden carriages rotted and they fell to the ground. They were worthless. Brass guns were highly sort after because of the value to brass. So these iron guns just lay on the ground or the beaches for centuries. The fact that they survived the salt air and sand is incredible considering that most of them are in very good condition. Some were used as bollards to protect the edge of buildings and many can be seen today around Bridgetown.

In 1985 the Director of the Maritime Museum in Bermuda, Dr. Richard Harris, came to Barbados for a holiday. Driving around he noticed the guns lying on the ground. He knew something about iron guns and he recognized most of them to be from the 17th century. He eventually arrived in the Author's office and poured his heart out at the neglect he had witnessed. The Author was persuaded to start lifting the guns into a central location. A Mr. Charles Trollope, an expert on old English guns, came out from England and between him and his wife they measured, identified and photographed every single gun. It soon became apparent that we had a quite remarkable collection. The question then was, where were the guns going to be displayed. Running along the walls of St. Ann's Fort was the old naval magazine. During the Napoleonic Wars the British fleet could not be based in the islands because many of them were in the hands of the French. Barbados became the Naval Headquarters in the Caribbean, with the dockyard and fleet in Carlisle Bay. In order to keep the gun powder dry for the ships, the naval magazine was built in 1800. It was an absolute natural location for the collection. On the 16th April 2004 the Rt. Hon. Owen Arthur, Prime Minister of Barbados, officially opened the National Armoury, the home of the Gun Collection.

*Official Opening of
the Barbados National
Armoury, 16th April
2004
Photo BDF Collection*

*The Prime Minister, The Rt. Hon. Owen Arthur,
arriving with the BDF Chief of Staff,
Col A. Quintyne and the author.
Photo BDF Collection*

*The Prime Minister unveiling
Elizabethan cannon of 1600,
the only one known to exist
anywhere in the world
Photo BDF Collection*

*The Prime Minister being briefed by the author
on a Commonwealth cannon of 1652
with Cromwell Republican Arms
on it. One of only two known to exist.
The British High Commissioner HE
Mr. John White and Colonel A.E. Quintyne,
Chief of Staff are also in the photograph
Photo BDF Collection*

*Nelson's secret weapon, a
24 Pdr Carronade top
deck gun on a swivel.
It could inflict great
damage on mast rigging
and personnel.
Photo BDF Collection*

*Some 17th century guns
Photo BDF Collection*

*Demi Culverin or 9 Pounder,
length 10', cast by John
Browne circ 1678.
Tudor Rose & Crown
Royal Cypher
Photo Author's collection*

*24 Pounder on its
original carriage dated
1810 and made by the
Carron Company of
Scotland and seen on
the Garrison Savannah
Photo Author's collection*

Denmark Fort, Speightstown
A 24 Pdr with original
carriage mounted on a slide
on wheels. The gun could
engage a moving target.
Photo Author's collection

8" Rifled Muzzle
Loader of 1870 with its
carriage and slide on
wheels. Photo taken at
Fort Charles after the
gun site had been
abandoned circa 1900.
Photo Author's collection

CHAPTER SEVENTEEN

THE BARBADOS LEGION AND
THE BARBADOS POPPY LEAGUE

The Barbados Legion and Poppy League are two separate organizations with a single purpose that is "to ensure that no ex-serviceman or woman shall be without help if in need". The two organizations deal specifically with ex-service personnel and therefore should be included in any military history of Barbados.

After the end of the First World War (1914 - 1918) poppy flowers grew in profusion over the battlefields of France and Belgium and became the symbol of remembrance for those who had been killed. Funds raised from the sale of artificial poppies every year finance the assistance given to those service persons in need.

In 1923 the Barbados Poppy Day League was formed at the instigation of Sir Charles O'Brien, the Governor at that time. Two stalwart ladies, Miss Dolly Hutson and Miss Daisy Yearwood, were the driving force behind the Committee. The funds collected were sent to a central account in London for distribution throughout the Commonwealth, including Barbados. However this system was soon changed and funds collected in Barbados were retained in order to assist the needy Barbadians. Throughout the years volunteers have worked tirelessly to raise the necessary funds and no more so than Lady Hyacinth Burton whose devotion to the League deserves special comment.

In 1945, at the end of the Second World War, the number of ex-servicemen and women in need increased dramatically and the Poppy League was unable to cope. In 1954 Colonel J. O. Connell went to London to discuss the formation of a Barbados Legion to be affiliated to the Royal British legion. This link was confirmed when in 1957 the Barbados Legion was formed. After that date the Poppy League was responsible for raising funds which were handed over to the Legion for distribution. It was thought that with the passing of the years, and with the legionnaires growing older, the organization would fade away. However, during the 1990s there was a surprising rejuvenation of the Legion. This was due to the following factors:-

a. The purchase by Government of the Main Guard on the Garrison Savannah as the headquarters of the Legion and the Poppy League.

b. The creation in 1990 of a new appointment on a permanent basis of a Garrison Secretary to co-ordinate the activities of both the Legion and the Poppy League.

*Members of the Legion attending a Drumhead
Service at the Main Guard*

c. Members of the Barbados Defence Force due for retirement were encouraged to join, thus bringing a younger element into the Legion.

The author became the first Garrison Secretary in 1990 and handed over to Lieut-Colonel F. E. Gittens in 1999. Gradually over the 1990s the income through sale of poppies increased and since the year 2000 the sum of BD$ 150,000 has been handed over to the Legion every year.

The Drumhead Service
at the Main Guard on
21 August 2005
L - R: Capt. P. Short,
Mrs. Blair, The Rt. Hon.
Tony Blair, Prime Minister
of Great Britain, The Rt.
Hon. Owen Arthur, Prime
Minister of Barbados and
His Excellency
Sir Clifford Husbands,
Governor General

The Main Guard with its conference room and its ability to host conferences, lectures and social occasions fostered the growth of an "Espirit de Corps" which was very evident in the early 21st century. In 2007 there are 412 legionnaires and the President is Lieut-Colonel F. E. Gittens, MVO, BSS, MSM. In 1999 the Barbados Legion hosted the British Commonwealth Ex-Services League's (BCEL) Tri-annual Conference. This was the first time a small country had been given the honour to do so. One hundred and twenty delegates together with their spouses, from 53 Commonwealth countries, gathered in Barbados. HRH Prince Philip, The Duke of Edinburgh, as Patron of the League was in attendance. The conference was hailed as an unqualified success. The future of legions world wide came under discussion and it was hoped that some formula could be adopted so that legions would be able to play a future part in helping needy ex-service personnel.

Visit of HRH The Prince Edward, 15th May 2003. The Prince meeting members of the Legion Council
L-R: Capt. P. Short, President, Lt-Col Springer, Warren Alleyne, Carl Ford, Gordon Hamilton,
George Brown, Patrick Manning, Major The Rev. M. Springer, Derek Davies.

BCEL Conference Delegates to the Tri-annual Conference of the BCEL held in Barbados in 1999. Seated in the centre is HRH The Duke of Edinburgh, on his right General Burgess, President BCEL, and on his left Captain P. Short, President of the Barbados Legion
Photo Brooks La Touche

HRH The Duke of Edinburgh being welcomed to the Officers' Mess of the Barbados Defence Force on the occasion of the British Commonwealth Ex Services League tri-annual conference 1999. Capt. P. Short, Sir Clyde Gollop and the author are in the picture.
Photo Felix Kerr

CHAPTER EIGHTEEN

THE BARBADOS
MILITARY CEMETERY

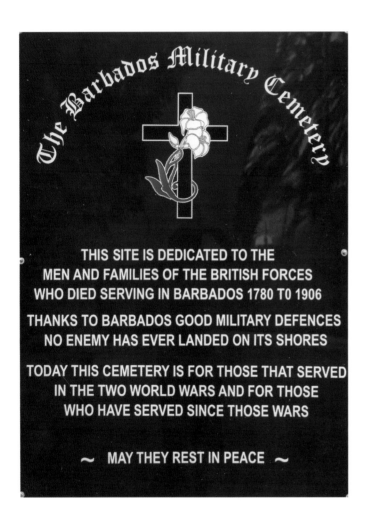

The Military Cemetery is not only an historic site but also an on going cemetery where ex-serviceman and women may be buried if they so wish. In 1780 the first British Regiment arrived in Barbados as part of what was to become a permanent Garrison for 125 years. There was no medical answer to yellow fever spread by the mosquito and thousands of British soldiers throughout the Caribbean died of the disease. In Barbados there was no specific area for them to be buried so the area between Charles Fort and St. Ann's Fort was selected as the burial ground. Up to 1780 the Militia men were buried in their parishes and there had been no need for a military cemetery.

In 1920, fifteen years after the last British soldiers had left, the oil refinery was allocated the land on which the graves were sited. Bulldozers moved in and flattened the land and the headstones to build the oil tanks. A group of concerned individuals saw what was happening and raised enough money to build a wall around what was left. That then became the Military Cemetery. Unfortunately the group ran out of funds and the area quietly reverted to bush but not before those same people gathered together all the headstones they could find outside the wall and made a cenotaph of them inside the cemetery. In 1975, under the initiative of the Barbados Regiment, the Barbados Military Cemetery Association was formed. Together with the Parks and Beaches Organization the cemetery was transformed from a wilderness to a landscaped garden. In 1981 the Cemetery was rededicated in the presence of the then Governor General, Sir Deighton Ward. The Cross of Sacrifice and the Sword were unveiled the next year. Burials of ex-servicemen and women have been taking place there ever since.

In this photograph are the graves of RN Engineer James Abbott and Sub lieutenant Taitt of HMS Rover. Both died on 18th June 1876 of Yellow Fever.

This headstone was erected in memory of James Sims, Naval Schoolteacher. He was to accompany two Royal Princes on a world tour on HMS Bacchante but fell ill and died in Barbados on 1st January 1880. The two Princes, Prince Albert and Prince George, attended the funeral in the Military Cemetery.

The unveiling of the Cross of Sacrifice by Governor General Sir Deighton Ward, 1982
assisted by Brigadier R.E.C. Lewis, Chief of Staff
Photo BDF Collection

Cenotaph displaying headstones found outside the cemetery when the oil refinery was built Photo Felix Kerr

HRH The Princess Ann, The Princess Royal, visited the cemetery in 1993. Colonel D. Maynard, acting Chief of Staff and the author are in the photograph. Photo BDF Collection

Memorial to Barbadian Merchant Seamen lost at sea in World War Two
(Photo Author's collection)

In 2002 it was pointed out to the Legion that there was no memorial to the Barbadian Merchant Seamen who lost their lives in World War Two. Their names were not recorded on the Cenotaph because they were civilian not servicemen although they were always in the front line. The Legion obtained the names of the seamen, acquired a large anchor (thanks to Esso Caribbean), mounted it on an impressive plinth and had the names inscribed on it. They are now remembered every year on Remembrance Day, November 11th.

The memorial headstone to Errol Barrow in the Military Cemetery
Photo Felix Kerr

APPENDIX

APPENDIX 1
CHARTER OF BARBADOS (1652)

On the 17th of January 1652, the following Articles were ratified:

The Charter of Barbados, or Articles of Agreement, had, made, and concluded on the 11th day of January 1652, by and between the Commissioners of the Right Honorable the Lord Willoughby of Parham of the one part, and the Commissioners in the behalf of the Commonwealth of England, of the other part in order to the Rendition of the Island of Barbados. And are as followeth:-

1. That a liberty of conscience in matters of religion be allowed to all, excepting such tenents as are inconsistent to a civil government; and that laws be put in execution against blasphemy, atheism, and open scandalous living, seditious preaching, or unsound doctrine sufficiently proved against him.

2. That the Courts of Justice shall continue, and all judgments and orders therein be valid, until they be reversed by due form of law.

3. That no taxes, customs, imports, loans, or excise shall be laid, nor levy made on any the inhabitants of this island without their consent in a General Assembly.

4. That no man shall be imprisoned or put out of his possession of land and tenements which he has by any former warrant, or title derived from it, or other goods or chattels whatsoever, without due proceedings according to the known Laws of England, and statutes and customs of this island in the Courts of Justice here first had, and judgment for the same obtained, and execution from thence awarded.

5. That all suits between party and party, and criminal and common pleas be determined here, and none be compelled to go into England to assert or defend their titles to any estate which they have here, without the consent of the General Assembly.

6. That an Act of Indemnity be with all convenient speed passed in the Parliament of England, to save, keep harmless and unquestionable all and every the inhabitants of this island that are comprised in these Articles, for or concerning any act or thing whatsoever done by them, or any of them at any time or in any place; or words spoken by them, or any of them before the date of these Articles, and that they be cleared, acquitted and discharged thereof for ever, in respect of the public power, as of any particular person concerning damage, or loss which they have received by reason of the present differences; and until the said Act come hither, an Instrument of Indemnity to all such comprised in these Articles to the purpose aforesaid, be assigned by Sir George Ayscue and the other Commissioners, and the said Act together with the said Instrument of Indemnity may be received into the Assembly here, and filed among the records, and that it be represented by Sir George Ayscue and the Commissioners to the Parliament of England, or the Council of State established by the authority of the Parliament: that an Act made on the 3rd day of October 1650, whereby the inhabitants have been declared traitors, may upon this accord be taken off the file from among the records.

7. That all and every the inhabitants of this island comprised in these Articles be restored to all their lands and possessions, goods and moneys which they have in England, Scotland or Ireland.

8. That no oaths, covenants, or engagements whatsoever be imposed upon the inhabitants of this island, who receive the benefit of these Articles against their consciences.

9. That all port-towns and cities under the Parliament's power shall be open unto the inhabitants of this island in as great a freedom of trade as ever, and that no companies be placed over them, nor the commodities of the island be ingrossed into private men's hands, and that all trade be free with all nations that do trade and are in amity with England.

10. That whereas the excise upon strong liquor was laid for the payment of public debts, and other public uses; it is therefore agreed that the Lord Willoughby of Parham, and all employed by him, and all other persons whatsoever, shall be acquitted and discharged from the payment of any public debts, and that the same be discharged by the said excise, and such other ways as the General Assembly shall think fit; provided that care and respect therein be had to such as have eminently suffered in their estates.

11. That all persons be free at any time to transport themselves and estates when they think fit, first setting up their names, according to the custom of this island.

12. That all persons on both sides be discharged and set free with the full benefit of enjoying these Articles, and that all horses, cattle, servants, negroes and other goods whatsoever, be returned to their right owners, except such servants as had freedom given them, and came on board before Saturday the third of January.

13. That such particular persons as are in this island, together with Sir Sydenham Pointz, who have estates in Antegoa, may peaceably return thither, and there enjoy the benefit of these Articles.

14. That for a certain time all executions be stopped, sufficient caution being given, that at the expiration of it payment be made, and that the Commissioners, together with the General Assembly, be judges of the time and caution.

15. That the three small vessels or barks now on ground before the Bridgetown do remain to their owners, and have liberty to go to any port laden.

16. That the Lord Willoughby of Parham have all his lands, rents, or estate whatsoever real and personal in England (without any fine or composition paid) restored to him, or his assigns, free from all incumbrances laid on the same by the Parliament of England, or any by them authorised since the time of its first seizure or sequestration; and that what settlements the said Lord Willoughby of Parham has made at Surinam, or any other he shall make on any part of the main of Guiana, shall be by him enjoyed and kept without any disturbance either of himself or those that shall accompany him thither, and that he has free liberty to bring servants from any part of England or Ireland, and that his plantation in Antegoa according to the bounds already laid out be reserved to him; and that what state soever of right doth belong unto the said Lord Willoughby of Parham in this island of Barbados be to him entirely preserved.

17. That all such persons of this island or elsewhere, whose estates have been sequestered or detained from them upon the public difference be forthwith restored to their plantations, goods or estates in the island.

18. That the Island of Barbados with all the forts, sconces and fortifications thereof, and all the artillery, all public arms and ammunitions be delivered up into the hands of Sir George Ayscue for the use of the States of England, before Monday twelve of the clock at noon, being the twelfth of this instant January, and that no garrison be kept here, but that all the forces shall be disbanded within twenty-four hours after the sealing of these Articles; and that for the safety of the island, the militia shall be disposed of as to the Parliament, Commissioners and future Governors shall seem fit; these Articles not to be construed to take away the private arms of any particular person within the island.

19. That the government of this island be by a Governor, Council and Assembly, according to the ancient and usual custom here: that the Governor be appointed by the States of England, and from time to time received and obeyed here, the Council be by him chosen, and an Assembly by a free and voluntary election of the freeholders of the island in the several parishes; and the usual custom of the choice of the Council be represented by the Commissioners to the Parliament of England, or to the Council of State established by authority of the Parliament, with the desires of the inhabitants for the confirmation thereof for the future.

20. And whereas, it has been taken into serious consideration, that the main and chief cause of our late troubles and miseries has grown by loose, base and uncivil language, tending to sedition and derision, too commonly used among many people here: it is therefore further agreed that at the next General Assembly a strict law be made against all such persons, with a heavy penalty to be inflicted upon them that shall be guilty of any reviling speeches of what nature soever, by remembering or raveling into former differences, and reproaching any man with the cause he has formerly defended.

21. It is agreed that the Articles may with all convenient speed be presented to the Parliament of England, to be by them ratified and confirmed to all intents, constitutions and purposes.

22. It is further agreed that all laws made heretofore by General Assemblies, that are not repugnant to the Laws of England, shall be good, except such as concern the present differences.

23. That the Right Honorable the Lord Willoughby of Parham have free liberty to go into England, and there stay or depart at his pleasure without having any oath or engagement put upon him, he acting or attempting nothing prejudicial to the State or Commonwealth of England.

In witness whereof we the Commissioners appointed by the Lord Willoughby of Parham, have hereunto set our hands and seals, this 11th day of January 1652.

Thomas Modyford,	Richard Pearse,
John Collet,	Charles Pym,
Daniel Searle,	Thomas Ellis,
Michael Pack.	William Byam.

Commissioners appointed by authority of the Commonwealth of Barbados.	Commissioners appointed for the Lord Willoughby and Island of England.

By the Governor

"It is my pleasure that the above written Articles be published by the several ministers in this island.

Given under my hand this 17th day of January 1652."

George Ayscue.

"This is a true copy with the original attested by me."

Jo. Jennings.

Clerk of the Assembly

APPENDIX 2

EYEWITNESS REPORT OF ADMIRAL de RUYTER'S ATTACK (1665)

A true relation of the fight at the Barbados, between the fforts and shipping there of the English, and De Ruyter Admirall of the Dutch the 20th of Aprill 1665. Observed by the Mast'r of the Ketch Hopewell (bound for Bristoll,) who was then riding the outmost vessel of the whole English ffleete and took p'ticular notice of the whole transfarrous.

About 6 of the clock in the morning, there was a report of De Ruyters coming and aboute 10 of the clock wee saw him with his whole ffleete which consisted of 14 sayle, and when hee came by the ffort, hee did not fire one gun until hee came at the Gifts stourne. Then hee fired a whole volley of small shott, and his broade side and soe did all the rest. Then the ffort and shipping fired at him, and they shot away all his foresayle, and the Vice Admirall lost his mayneyard and two other lost theyre topsayles.

11:aclock-2: *De Ruyter stayed, and in staying, was shot downe his mayne yard, and made some of them lie on the careonne to stopp her leakes.*

12:aclock-3: *De Ruyter fired his broade side agayne, and 6 of the rest, and wee did make two of them lie on the careen to stop theyre leakes.*

1:aclock-4: *De Ruyter stayed agayne, and hee could hardly wend cleare of the shippe Allen of Poole, and then hee was not so fair from mee as wire the length of his shippe. I did see him on the poope with a rame in one hand and a ruttle axe in the other, and as he stayed I did see most of his quarter carried away.*

2:aclock-5: *After De Ruyter was turned again, hee did fire his broad side and so did the rest of the fleete.*
6: Our shipps shott again at De Ruyter, and shott one of his boats at his sterne and sunk her, also wee did rend one of his rear admiralls maynesayles out of the roapes, and did place 3 shotts in one of the vice admiralls, and layde him on one side, with which I doo believe hee had much water in his hould.

3:aclock-7: *I did see all De Ruyters sterne to bee carr'd in, that it was soo wide as a barnes doore, and after that shott, they did not fire any more, for I did suppose De Ruyter was then killed.*

4:aclock-8: *After this De Ruyters shippe did bare up and come too an Ancker and all his fleete, and they did take downe all their red cullers and put up blew, and then they did all repayre on board De Ruyters shippe as I suppose to hould a Councell of War.*

5:aclock-9: *Thay did ride the spare of a houre, and then they weighed Ancker and did bare before the wind and when they weare of they did lie and mend theyre sayles, - I saw four of them lie on the Careene and stop theyre leakes.*

6:aclock-10: *They went away in the confuseds manner that possible could bee.*

Three days after wee did heare they weard at Martinora.

APPENDIX 3

1780 LIST OF FORTS & GUNS (CANNON) IN BARBADOS

A TOTAL OF 40 FORTS & GUNS AND 364 GUNS (CANNON)

OISTINS DIVISION

Oistins Fort	32
Kendal's Battery (Bty)	6
Maxwell's Bty	7
Frere's Bty	7

Total   52 Guns

ST. MICHAEL'S DIVISION

Charles Fort	42
St. Ann's Castle	23
Ormond's Bay	10
Willoughby Fort	16
James Fort	9
Grenville Fort	11
Hallet's Bay	2
Yacht Bty	7
Valiant Royalist (Bty)	5
Britton's Hill Bty	9

Total 134 Guns

ST. JAMES DIVISION

James Fort	20
Barbados Bty	5
Holders Bty	5
Howe's Bty	3
Meeting Bty	6
Denmark Fort	9

Total   48 Guns

LEEWARD DIVISION

Orange Fort	14
Dover Castle	8
Hayward's Bty	6
Hall's Hill Bty	2
Six Men's Fort	11
Lascelles Bty	3
Trents Bty	6
Church Bty	9
George's Bty	9
Clarendon Bty	6
Royal George	3
Margaret's Bty	8
Rochester Bty	2
Royal Charlotte's Bty	3
Thornhill Bty	7
Kyd's Hill Bty	6
Colleton Hill Bty	2
Rupert's Bty	6
Half Moon Bty	9
Maycock's Fort	10

Total   130 Guns

APPENDIX 4
MAP OF
GARRISON
HISTORIC AREA

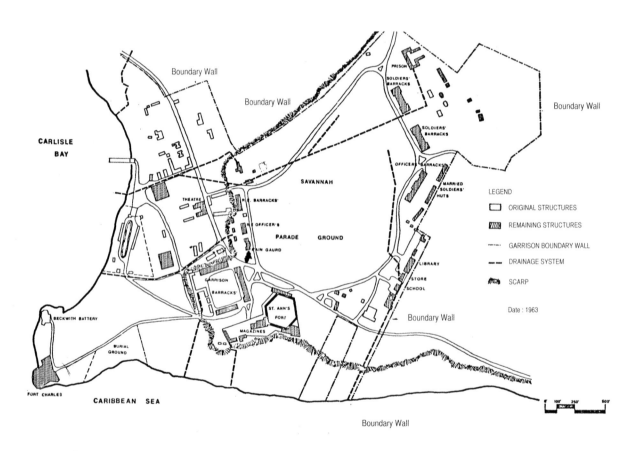

APPENDIX 5

POEM BY B. WILLIAMS OF 2ND W.I.R.

**The presentation of the Special Ashanti Star
to the Left wing 2nd Batt. West India Regt.**
BY HIS EXCELLENCY GOVERNOR CARDEW, C.M.G.
Sierra Leone, September, 25th 1896

Second West boys hail with delight
For a Kingdom won without fight
You all shall wear this Special Star
For duty you performed so far.

Akroful Stagnant water will tell
This Star on your breast is honoured well
Dunkwa's Villagers too have known
How you all have weary grown.

Mansu, Suta, Prashu's woods
Witness you all marched very good
Steep up brave Boys, take this gift from your Queen
For that great expedition you all have been.

Fumsu, Brafu Edru, Adansi Hill
Will remind you of hardships you all fulfil
For many miles far from home
In forest dark you all did roam.

The Star will tell of the danger you face
In Kumassi that dark heathen place
Three Cheers for brave General Scott
Who led you through that horrid spot.

Take now this Star from the Governor's hands
Among Staff Corps you took your stand
And when the enemies rail once more
Be up and take the gifts in Store.

You lose Prince Henry so very bold
The Star a mourning you are told
And when you wear the Ashanti Star
Its honoured well without a bar.

The Star is Symbolized of a cross
The woods passed possessed much moss
The many hardships you subdue
The Queen's honour is justly due.

The Star you wear is one of peace
From bloodshed your hands did cease
So when you wear this Peaceful Star
It's grudged by some without a bar.

Second West Boys hail with delight
For Ashanti subdue without fight
And when you think of where you been
Be cheerful to obey your Gracious Queen.

God Save the Queen.

Composed by B WILLIAMS

2nd W I Regiment

BIBLIOGRAPHY

Alleyne, Warren   Barbados at War 1939 – 1945, Warren Alleyne, 1999

**Alleyne, Warren
& Sheppard, Jill**   The Barbados Garrison and its Buildings,
McMillan Education Ltd., 1990

Caulfield, Col. J.E.   One Hundred Years History of the 2nd Batt. West India Regiment,
Forster Groom & Co., 1899

Darnell, N. D.   Cavaliers and Roundheads of Barbados, Argosy Press,
Guyana, 1887

Dyde, Brian   The Empty Sleeve, Hansib Caribbean, Antigua, 1997

Goddard, Richard   George Washington's Visit to Barbados 1751, Coles Printery, 1997

Ligon, Richard   True and Exact History of the Island of Barbadoes 1657,
Edited & annotated by Edward J. Hutson, Barbados National Trust,
Barbados, 2000

Schomburgk, Robert H.   The History of Barbados, Frank Cass, London,
New impression 1971

Taylor, S.A.G.   The Western Design, Institute of Jamaica, 1963

Watson, Elvey   Carib Regiment of World War II, Vantage Press, New York, 1964

Hutson. J. Edward   The English Civil War in Barbados 1650-1652,
Coles printery Ltd., 2001